Dedication

To Craig, Nikki, and Grandma Antonia Flatoff.

Acknowledgments

Thank you, Craig, for allowing me all the time I needed to research and write this book. A big thanks to Nikki for joining me on investigations and also for proofreading. Thank you Wayne Hackler, Gary Westerlund, Abbie Tippit, and the rest of the Madison Researchers Into The Paranormal team for your time and input.

Thanks to the many contributors who graciously gave of their time (and in many cases, photos), especially: Ruth Forrest Glenn, Makenzie Barron, Cyndal Gilson, Cody Ferkey, Kennadie Jenner, Jimmy Jenner, Terre Sims, Vicky Elsing, Judith Ulch, Soniya Davis, Kimi Matz, Randy Austin, Patricia Ralls, and Priscilla Ralls. I couldn't have done it without you!

Finally, thanks to my parents, George and Audrey Ferkey, and to my editor, Dinah Roseberry. You're the best!

The Ghosts of Madison, Wisconsin

Sherry Strub

Schiffer Publishing Ltd®

4880 Lower Valley Road, Atglen, Pennsylvania 19310

Designed by Stephanie Daugherty
Type set in A Charming Font Expanded/
NewBskvll BT

ISBN: 978-0-7643-3072-8
Printed in China

Schiffer Books are available at special
discounts for bulk purchases for sales
promotions or premiums. Special editions,
including personalized covers, corporate
imprints, and excerpts can be created in
large quantities for special needs. For more
information contact the publisher:

Published by Schiffer Publishing Ltd.
4880 Lower Valley Road
Atglen, PA 19310
Phone: (610) 593-1777;
Fax: (610) 593-2002
E-mail: Info@schifferbooks.com

Please visit our web site catalog at
www.schifferbooks.com

We are always looking for people to write
books on new and related subjects. If you have
an idea for a book, please contact us at the
above address.

This book may be purchased from the
publisher. Include $5.00 for shipping. Please
try your bookstore first. You may write for a
free catalog.

In Europe, Schiffer books are distributed by:
Bushwood Books
6 Marksbury Ave.
Kew Gardens
Surrey TW9 4JF England
Phone: 44 (0)208 392-8585
Fax: 44 (0)208 392-9876
E-mail: Info@bushwoodbooks.co.uk
Website: www.bushwoodbooks.co.uk

Free postage in the UK. Europe: air mail at
cost. Try your bookstore first.

Contents

Introduction
Madison's Ghosts

Madison is unlike anywhere else. The city and area around it contain the world famous, or soon-to-be-world-famous, Capital Brewery in Middleton, splendid-to-behold Capitol building, and Henry Vilas Zoo—one of the few zoos in the country that is still free to attend. Then there's the slightly less conventional Dr. Evermor's Forevertron outside of Madison, House on the Rock with its bizarre doll collection, carousel, and room that goes off the edge of a cliff (haunted Taliesen is just down the road) in Spring Green, and Gobbler Restaurant in Johnson Creek—just to name a few places and things you really ought to check out.

When I hear the word Madison, the phrase "twenty-six miles, surrounded by reality" comes to mind. That number, of course, has a wide variance, depending upon where you hear it. Sometimes Madison makes me think of Mad Town, Mad City, or the City of Four Lakes. For those not familiar with the fab four successive lakes of the Yahara River, they are: Lake Mendota, Lake Monona, Lake Waubesa, and Lake Kegonsa (although Waubesa and Kegonsa aren't technically in Madison). Madison is many things to many people; Madison is many things to one person!

The Capitol, located in downtown Madison, is located on an isthmus between Lakes Mendota and Monona. The Capitol also has the only granite dome in the nation. The land around the Capitol was once surrounded by thousands of effigy mounds built by Native Americans; now only a few remain.

Most often, though, I think of diversity when I hear the word Madison. Wisconsinites are rabid Badgers fans, but don't think sports are all Madisonians have on their brains. In 2004, *Forbes* magazine reported that Madison has the highest percentage of Ph.D.s in the nation. In 2006, *Forbes* listed Madison as number 31 in the top 200 metro areas for "Best Places for Business and Careers."

Others remember Madison for its eccentric, iconic characters that were once a part of the city's everyday scene: Tunnel Bob, Piccolo

Guy, Scanner Dan, and Art the Window Washer (who spawned a T-shirt craze).

Madison has one of the most extensive bike trail systems in the nation. Because of its active cyclist culture, it's likely you'll see at least a few cyclists riding through the city, even in the winter. You might even see a cyclist of the ghostly persuasion pass you by if you happen to be walking along the shores of Lake Mendota on a late summer night!

State Street, linking the University of Wisconsin Madison (UWM) campus with the State Capitol square, has just about everything you could ever want within its boundaries: restaurants, shops, cafés, taverns. Even cooler—only pedestrians, bikes, buses, and emergency and delivery vehicles are allowed on State Street. And while you're there, check out the Capitol, which many say is inhabited by a ghost or two.

Madison holds a wide variety of attractions and experiences for the resident and visitor: the Dane County Farmer's Market held around the Capitol Square in the summer, boasts 160 local vendors. There are also free concerts performed by the Wisconsin Chamber Orchestra, the Great Taste of the Midwest craft beer festival, Rhythm and Booms fireworks celebration (an understatement), Kites on Ice held on Lake Mendota, UWM, Camp Randall Stadium, Chazen Museum of Art, Wisconsin Historical Society, and the Unitarian Meeting House.

Some famous Wisconsinites who were born near Madison or lived here are: actresses Tyne Daly and Gena Rowlands, actor Chris Farley, speed skater Eric Heiden, authors Laura Ingalls Wilder and Thornton Wilder, and the first woman to win the Iditarod Trail Sled Dog Race, Libby Riddles. Talk about an impressive list!

The University of Wisconsin Madison, in addition to having numerous ghosts in residence on campus, is one of the most well-know, well-respected universities in the United States, both academically and because of its athletics program. But that's not all it's know for: It has two rather large student-driven gatherings, the State Street Halloween Party and the Mifflin Block Party. The State Street Halloween Party, named "Freakfest On State Street," is filled with activities and performances by bands. Partiers from all around Wisconsin drive to Madison to join in the festivities. How many apparitions seen that night by party-goers are real or imagined?

Sports Illustrated named Madison the number one college sports town in 2003. No surprise there. The only surprise is that Madison isn't number one every year—school spirit just doesn't get any stronger. Either do the spirits that linger in and around Camp Randall Stadium. (And a disappearing corpse that was spotted nearby!)

The first commercial districts of Madison, King Street and the East Main and South Pinckney Street sides of the Capitol Square, still have fine examples of early architecture. They're so nice, in fact, that some residents never leave the buildings they worked in, despite the fact they died.

The first residential districts north of the Square, such as Gorham, Gilman, and Langdon Streets, are other places that the ghosts of Madison call home.

But don't think the smaller communities around Madison are slouches when it comes to ghosts. Some of these ghosts are known around the world—and they're just as unique as the ghosts who haunt Madison's city limits.

So get comfortable, make yourself a cup of coffee or tea, open a health drink, pop the top of a soft drink, or pour yourself a long tall, glass of milk, and get to know some of the Ghosts of Madison, Wisconsin.

Haunts, Haunts,
and More Haunts!

𝔖anitarium

Northport Office of the Dane County Department of Human Services, formerly the Lake View Tuberculosis Sanatorium.

T he current Northport Office of the Dane County Department of Human Services was once the Lake View Tuberculosis Sanatorium. Ghost hunters call it the sanitarium now, although the correct spelling should be "sanatorium" to follow the original spelling of Lake View Tuberculosis Sanatorium.

It's quite easy to find. Located on 1202 Northport Drive/Hwy. 113, it literally seems to jump into your line of vision, no matter what lane of traffic you're in, from its monstrous perch at the top of the hill. It's the veritable definition of the word imposing.

Sledding down Sanitarium Hill.

In the winter, people sled down the huge hill, many unaware of the haunted woods above them.

The sanitarium (especially the woods and cemetery at the top of the hill) is at the top of the wish list of professional investigative teams and amateurs alike. Some say the ghosts there are the result of the many that undoubtedly lost their lives at the sanitarium; others believe the place is haunted because of its location on a hill overlooking water. This would indicate that the spirits here are Native American.

One thing that makes this site so unusual is the number of people who believe the ghosts of the sanitarium chased or forced them out. Worse—many believe the evil spirits of the sanitarium followed them home.

Spirits in the Cemetery and the Woods

The first story comes from a woman who can "feel" the presences of spirits. She's visited the sanitarium a half dozen times and plans more trips in the future. She says she believes the building itself is not haunted, but says it gives off a strong psychic vibration. She believes the buildings around the sanitarium that have been called haunted by many, are like the sanitarium—not haunted.

However, she believes the cemetery and woods exhibit definite signs of psychic activity which include cold drafts that envelop you, mists that show up on film that are not there when you look at the cemetery or grounds in person, and also the sound of voices.

These voices are disturbing because, though they are low in volume, they send a chill through you. "The eastern end of the

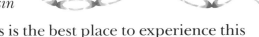

cemetery that borders the woods is the best place to experience this negative psychic energy," she says.

She believes the woods themselves are haunted by an angry presence. "Or evil," she says. Though she hasn't seen a ghost herself, others she's talked to have seen ghosts here. She thinks one explanation for the ghosts is the two outbuildings in the area which are now only foundations with smoke stacks. These ghosts might have spent time there in life, or passed away there. It's also rumored that the dead from the sanitarium were burned in the smoke stacks, and that the nurses' barracks, one of the buildings, was connected by an underground tunnel to the main building.

"The evil presence in the woods could have another explanation," she says. "I believe there is a good deal of satanic goings-on there. I've seen bones and clumps of hair on the ground that seemed to be in some sort of pattern."

Lots college kids go to the woods and cemetery to check out the site. "Be very careful if you decide to visit the woods and cemetery," she advises. "Come prepared for what you might encounter, human and otherwise."

The spirit(s) might linger with you longer than you would like.

It Yanked My Ponytail and Slapped Me!

"I'm probably the most skeptical person you ever met," Krystal M. says by way of introduction. "But I know what I felt and saw. It scared me so much, I'll never ever go back to that place." That *place* is the sanitarium.

Krystal moved to the area a year ago. She says she didn't believe in ghosts, but she didn't *not* believe in ghosts, either. Her cousin told her about the sanitarium and all the things that had happened to her when she'd been there. Her interest piqued, Krystal agreed to go with her cousin to visit the sanitarium woods.

They parked near the sanitarium a little before midnight. Krystal thought the idea of going there at midnight was a little hokey, but she's a black belt and felt certain she could take care of herself and her cousin should their plans go awry.

"We were just past the water tower, when my cousin—at least that's what I thought at the time—pulled my ponytail so hard, it actually yanked my head backward. I lost my balance and fell down. I immediately started yelling at my cousin, which in retrospect was

kind of stupid. She was a good yard in front of me. She couldn't have yanked my hair."

Krystal admits it freaked her out. She spun around but didn't see anything, even when she moved her flashlight all around her. As she turned to look at her cousin, she felt someone tap her on the shoulder—hard.

"My cousin must have seen the look on my face because she asked me what was wrong. I told her someone tapped me on the shoulder, expecting her to say, 'I told you so,' or something like that. Instead, her eyes got really big and she started running away from me."

This is where you or I might have turned tail and raced back to the car, but not Krystal. "That's when I got mad. I thought she was playing a trick on me, but then again, she looked really scared.

Water tower hidden in the sanitarium woods.

I remember thinking it was impossible for anyone to manufacture such a genuine look of fear."

Krystal turned around and found herself face to face with…well, she's still not quite sure. "It was human-sized, but like a gray mist in the darkness. And it was really close to me. The next thing I knew, it slapped me on the side of my face. The weird thing is, it really hurt." That's where all her martial arts training went out the window. "I turned around and ran after my cousin, screaming my head off."

She remembers that the air seemed to go really cold then, too. She also noticed a "stink" in the air that hadn't been there when they'd arrived. She says she still marvels that she could put one foot in front of the other because she was shaking so hard.

Krystal says she and her cousin stopped short in the cemetery. It was very quiet. She doesn't remember any kind of noise whatsoever. And just like that, a light rose from above a grave. It wasn't white or yellow like the light a flashlight might make; it was more of an orange-red color.

Neither of the women could move—or breathe. They watched the light head straight for them and then disappear into thin air. That might have been comforting, but for Krystal that was it. She'd heard and seen and felt more than she ever dreamed possible. She wanted to get away from the sanitarium, and fast.

Her cousin was quick to agree. They grabbed each other's hands and started back to the road. Neither of them said a word, but someone or something was still nearby. They kept hearing harsh whispering in their ears. They looked at each other, burst into tears, and started running back to the car.

But that wasn't the end of the story. Sitting in the locked car, sobbing and shaking, they heard the low sound of whispering again. They both looked at each other, frowned, and looked out the car window.

On the side of the car closest to the woods, was that same blob of gray mist that had "slapped" Krystal when they were near the cemetery.

"I started screaming at my cousin to get us out of there. I stayed at her house for the rest of the week. I still get nightmares about the mist and I swear sometimes I still hear that horrible whispering in my ear."

When asked if she thinks the ghostly presence that assaulted her at the sanitarium is still with her, an angry look flits across her face.

"I pray to God that it went back to the sanitarium where it belongs. I didn't do anything to it, so why would it still be here with me?"

I guess only the ghostly presence has the answer to that haunting question.

Orton Park

Orton Park, Madison.

Few would argue this park looks like your typical neighborhood park. Its asphalt path cuts through trees, past an inviting gazebo. This might be an ordinary park at first glance, except for the fact that it was once the final resting place of many Madisonians. Did I say final? What I meant to say was second to final resting place. This plaque on the park grounds proves it.

Many that visit the park, including myself, experience a feeling of unease on the grounds. When you stand near a couple of the biggest trees, the feeling grows from unease to downright creepiness.

Here's a little about the park. Block 180, as it was known back in the 1840s, was the Village of Madison's first formal cemetery. Until June of 1866, the good citizens of the village were buried there—246 to be exact. At the time, there were no trees in the cemetery, and because a fence cost a few dollars (at the time a lot of money), one was never purchased. Cows and other animals walked, and who knows what else, on the graves and marred the sacred site.

Madison began to grow at a much faster rate than anyone back then anticipated. It was obvious the small cemetery, just four square acres (one city block), would never hold all the future graves. Within six years, local papers were asking for a new cemetery. The current site of Forest Hill was selected, bought and paid for, and put into use in 1858. (Forest Hill also happens to h-h-haunted, too.)

At that time, the city council prohibited any more burials in the village "city block" cemetery. As you might imagine, as Madisonians died and were laid to rest at Forest Hill, family members who had been laid to rest at the village cemetery were taken out of the cemetery and interred in Forest Hill near their families.

Orton Park plaque.

Starting in September of 1859, the remaining bodies in the village cemetery were removed and interred in Forest Hill in what would be their final resting place. Unfortunately, records identifying who had been buried in the village cemetery were nonexistent, and many of the wooden markers, that had identified the graves, had rotted and deteriorated. Who were these unfortunate souls? The only thing we know for sure is many of these unknowns from the village cemetery are buried in unmarked graves in Forest Hill.

In December of 1877, the village cemetery was sold to John Schlimgen and Anton Steinle for $1,105; they planned on converting it into a beer garden. But not for long. Public outcry caused the city to buy the block from the two entrepreneurs. Harlow S. Orton, who became Madison's fifteenth mayor in 1877, cast the deciding vote in favor of purchasing the land to create a park. The park was later named after him. Orton's other claims to fame: He was dean of the UW law school from 1869 to 1874, and also served as associate justice of the state supreme court from 1878 until his death in 1895.

The story of how it evolved from cemetery to park ends there, but not the stories of ghosts and hauntings.

Madison's founding fathers—along with the body movers themselves—most likely thought, or at the very least hoped, they had moved all the bodies in the village cemetery to Forest Hill, but they didn't. That's why so many believe Orton Park is one of the most haunted places in Madison.

The trees in the park are most often mentioned as being haunted. Do they contain the spirits of those that were originally buried in the park? Others say they see phantom shapes looking around trees at them as they pass. A general feeling of unease is most often reported.

The Ghost In The Balcony

T he Majestic Theatre is one of Madison's historic landmarks and oldest running theatres. It was originally built in 1906; at that time it was a vaudeville that featured live performances. In 1925, the Majestic began playing movies for the princely sum of 25¢. *Dante's Inferno*, its first feature, was described as "the greatest thing of its kind ever shown in Madison."

The theater was once a dance club and even hosted a private birthday bash for a prominent Wisconsin Senator. It currently features concerts and performing arts venues and has become a hot spot for those wanting to see or hear their favorite artists live.

Many remember the Majestic as it was in the "old days." They remember the carpeted lobby and old water fountain and the quasi-boxes on either side of the balcony.

Some remember the strange feeling they sometimes got there. It's been described as "claustrophobic" and "as if someone was watching me, even when no one else was inside the theater."

Others remember the Majestic Theatre, located at 115 King Street, off the Capitol Square, as a place where a ghost hung out in the balcony.

The events of the story may have varied from employee to employee, but the subject of the story was always the same: A man in the back row of the balcony would wave to whomever happened to be down below cleaning. Another thing that was the same: The employee who saw the ghost was usually so shook up, he or she had to leave. In several cases the employee refused to work late at night, or alone, ever again.

One employee claims he was sweeping the aisles when he looked up and saw a man in the back row of the balcony. When he was finished, he went upstairs to tell the man he was closing up. As he approached the man from the stairs, which was the only entrance and exit to the balcony, he found the man had disappeared into thin air.

The next employee's story is out-and-out frightening. While cleaning, he got the feeling he was being watched. He hazarded a glance up and saw a man sitting in the back row of the theater. He

waved up at the man, no doubt thinking he was a customer. The man waved back.

End of story? I'm sure the employee wishes it were. As the man continued to wave, his arm began moving away from his body. The employee dropped what he was doing and raced from the building. This story is almost identical to a story told to me by a former UW Madison student who attended a movie there one evening long ago when she attended the university in the mid-1980s.

While the name of the movie escapes the alumni, the details of what happened during the film are inescapable. She had attended the foreign movie with a friend; neither had been drinking, but both saw the same "impossible" thing. In the middle of the movie, she told her friend she had to use the bathroom. As she got up to go, she glanced behind her and saw what looked like a "putty man" growing taller and taller in the balcony. Her friend looked up, saw the same thing and screamed.

Whether it was the scream, or something else, the putty man disappeared. The woman decided against using the bathroom. She and her friend left the theater as fast as they could. They later told the story about what happened to them to several friends. These friends said they had feelings of being watched there, too.

Club Majestic, as it was formerly known, closed its doors recently and reopened in the fall of 2007 as a live concert and performing arts venue. It's once again the Majestic Theatre.

Whether the ghost in the balcony is still there, is anyone's guess. The atmosphere has changed drastically since the 1980s and 1990s when sightings of the ghost were at their peak. Maybe the ghost decided to move on. Or maybe it's waiting to see if the latest changes to the more than 100-year-old building are to its satisfaction.

The Bar Next Door

The Bar Next Door, Madison.

The Bar Next Door, located at 232 E. Olin Avenue is a gorgeous, turreted brick building, built in 1929 as a roadhouse for the Touhey brothers. For those of you not familiar with the Touheys, they were the chief rivals of Al Capone. If the building looks a little like a fortress, you may be on to something. There are hidden compartments under the windowsills that just happen to be the right size to hold a Thompson submachine gun. The building is made of bulletproof brick more than a foot thick. Once upon a time, the building was the Wonder Bar, a reputed Chicago Mob hangout during Prohibition days.

The bar is a registered national historical place, so it must maintain its original façade. The interior walls are decorated with things from its time as a speakeasy. The cellar door is the portal to the tunnel system which leads to the lake; apparently mobs could never be too careful.

One ghostly occupant that has been seen moving a series of cigar boxes with phantom hands might well be a Touhey. Or if not a Touhey, maybe someone who was foolish enough to interfere with their bootlegging operation.

One patron of the bar said he's smelled the very distinct odar of cigar smoke when no one in the bar was smoking. He's also heard footsteps behind him, felt a presence, then turned around to see no one there.

Regulars call the ghost Joe. This same Joe is reportedly buried behind the fireplace in the second floor banquet room. His last name, surprise of surprises, is believed to be Touhey. Those that don't believe this to be a Touhey brother have a different theory. They think the dead man behind the fireplace is most likely

The Bar Next Door. A beautiful fortress.

someone who double-crossed the Touheys. The man behind the fireplace might not be the only body encased in The Bar Next Door's architecture. The amount of ghostly activity in the building suggests more than one ghost.

A paranormal investigative team recently investigated the establishment and found that one of the gas fireplaces was turned on when there was no way it could have turned itself on. People have also seen the apparition of a man in a trench coat.

Patrons of this historical building, as well as at least one manager, have heard footsteps descending the staircase, late at night. Apparently ghosts enjoy a drink once in a while, too.

Taliesen

Taliesen, Spring Green.

T aliesen means "shining brow" in Welsh—just in case you didn't know. Many know Taliesen as an incredible home perched on sandstone, designed by famed architect Frank Lloyd Wright. There is another Taliesen. This Taliesen has a history rife with adultery, arson, fire caused by lightning, fire caused by electric problems, murder, and incredibly, the robbing of Wright's body from the nearby cemetery.

When you learn more about Taliesen's history, you can't help but be impressed that no matter what happened to Wright, he kept plugging away. Many others might have fled or done something drastic to end their troubles.

Taliesen is built into a hill.

Many who live in Wisconsin have visited at least one of Wright's creations. I took a tour of the House on the Rock when I was a student as part of a class trip. As an adult, I visited the House on the Rock again and Taliesen for the first time. Like Wright's chameleon talents, the impressions you get each time you view one of his creations also change. The only thing that doesn't change is the sense of awe you feel.

Taliesen is located at Highways 23 and C, close to the town of Spring Green. If you drive by, you will likely see signs that indicate this is private property. You will also see water spilling over a dam near the entrance to the home, just a hint that this isn't your ordinary abode.

You might not call Taliesen a castle, but in a way, it is much more. Perched on a shelf of earth, Taliesen captures not only your glance, but your imagination. When you learn about the ghosts who reside there, it compels you to learn more about its history.

Taliesen is compelling even without its ghosts. It has been called a "living laboratory of architecture" because Wright and his acolytes were always tweaking things. You are struck by the low ceilings inside Taliesen, which make you want to sit down, for some odd reason. Even the furniture seems hand-selected by Wright. The views are perfect each time you sit.

Here's a little about the man responsible for this architectural wonder: Frank Lloyd Wright. He was born on June 8, 1867, in nearby Richland, Wisconsin. Anna Lloyd Jones, a schoolteacher, and William Carey Wright, a preacher and musician, were his parents.

During his youth, he spent many of his summers in the Richland area he considered home. The time he spent there made an impression on him; he incorporated the nature all around him in the designs of his early years.

Wright headed to Chicago in 1886 to pursue his dream—architecture. While in Chicago, he married Catherine Lee Tobin, built a home in Oak Park, and had four sons and two daughters. Wright and his wife parted ways in 1893.

This timeframe seems to be a turning point in Wright's life. In 1909, he went to Europe with an Oak Park woman named Mamah Borthwick Cheney, who happened to be the wife of one of his clients. Remember her; she's likely one of the ghosts that haunt Taliesen.

Wright's creation is a top tourist destination.

Wright returned to the United States with Mamah Borthwick Cheney in tow just a year later. Surprise (or not)! They returned to scandal and censure in Chicago. They didn't stay there for long. Borthwick Cheney was beautiful, independent, and strong-willed, just like Wright, who was known as an intellectual free-thinker. Apparently inspired, it was at this time that Wright began building Taliesen. This beautiful building was Wright's primary dwelling for the rest of his life.

Taliesen has a violent history. It's been leveled twice, once by lightning and once by arson. The arson, which killed Wright's mistress, her two children, house guests, and the man that set the fire, is believed to be the reason for the ghosts that inhabit Taliesen. It's also endured a number of other fires.

Wright was not one to fade into the woodwork. He had a mistress and was married three times in all; the first time to Catherine "Kitty" (Tobin) Wright, a socialite and social worker; the second time to Maude "Miriam" (Noel) Wright, an artist, and; the third time to dancer and writer, Olga Ivanovna "Olgivanna" (Lazovich Milanoff) Wright. He had eight children; actress Anne Baxter, who died in 1985, was Frank Lloyd Wright's granddaughter.

About the fire: When it destroyed part of Taliesen in 1914, Wright was in Chicago on business. The fire itself was pretty gruesome. It was also pretty sensational. Frank Lloyd Wright's cook (some say it was the gardener) gathered everyone together for lunch, locked all the doors and windows, set fire to the house, and then murdered six people in the dining room and the screened porch with a hatchet. Those killed included Wright's mistress, Mamah Borthwick Cheney, and her two small children.

The murderous rampage most likely wasn't the result of Frank Lloyd Wright and Borthwick Cheney's illicit romance. It turns out she often fired servants and staff members for very small offenses. The man who set the fire and committed the murders at Taliesen happened to be a former servant from Barbados.

After the fire, Wright returned to Taliesen and began rebuilding. Despite all the bad memories associated with the place, he spent most of the rest of his life there. When he died, he was buried in a nearby cemetery. Oddly, he didn't stay there.

More than twenty-five years after Wright's death, his body was taken from the cemetery by his fourth and final wife's friends after she

died. The reason? The fourth wife wanted Wright's body exhumed and cremated when she died so their ashes could be scattered together. When Wright's family ix-nayed the idea, the fourth wife's family went ahead and carried out her wishes anyway.

The smell of burnt wood can be smelled in Taliesen as you pass through the dining room. Many say they've seen shadows and have heard faint female voices inside the incredible interior. Small ghostly children wearing strange outfits have been seen on the grounds, and photographers have captured inexplicable mists on the hills of Taliesen. Many, including me, have experienced a strange feeling of unease in certain places in the house.

A cottage on the property, Tan-Y-Deri, is another place where ghostly sightings have been reported, and the ghost is described as wearing a long white gown. The ghost gives off peaceful vibes. Mrs. Borthwick Cheney? The doors and windows are said to open by themselves. Even when the cottage has been securely closed for the day, the next morning, doors are open.

Whether the ghosts who inhabit Taliesen and Tan-Y-Deri are Mamah Borthwick Cheney, her children, or Wright's last wife, there is little doubt ghosts do exist here.

Weary Road

Weary Road, Evansville.

Weary Road seems half ghost story and half urban legend. The road and the bridge, which is also said to be haunted, are located two miles east of Evansville on Highway 14.

Some of the many rumors feature a phantom train, strange and spook lights, and odd little beings in the trees alongside the road. Others have seen a green glow toward the end of the road. Which end? Which road? There are two Weary Roads—if you want to get technical.

And the green glow? It's said to be the ghost of Old Man Weary, the subject of two very different Old Man Weary stories.

They Said He Was a Pedophile

The first and shortest story about Old Man Weary has him pegged a pedophile because he "entertained" the local children. The story was just that, a story, yet a group of parents supposedly got together and burned his house down.

Turns out he had several children at his home when the blaze was set. Everyone was killed in the fire; later it was learned Old Man Weary was not a pedophile.

Of course the house no longer exists, but that doesn't stop visitors from parking near the spot where his driveway once was. Phantom cars and a ghostly motorcycle are said to have followed visitors on occasion. Who owned the vehicles before they became phantom? Everyone has a different answer. One good thing: The vehicles stop following you once you make a right hand turn. Apparently phantom vehicles don't have steering wheels.

Don't turn off your car or lights while you're on the bridge trying to outrun the phantom vehicle—it won't start again when you turn on the key. At least that's the story. There's also a side story to this story. A young man was said to have died car surfing on Weary Road. Could he be the phantom?

Visit Weary Road Three Times

In this story, Old Man Weary was a rich man who lived in a mansion with servants and a loving family. Despite all he had going for him, he was a cruel man who was only concerned with worldly possessions; he owned nearly all the land in the area.

Old Man Weary was hated by his family and the townsfolk alike. In this version, rich Old Man Weary was either tied to his bed and his estate set on fire, or Old Man Weary was murdered by his family, who then set the house on fire with him inside.

Teens who tell the story of Weary Road insist that you must visit the area three times before you witness anything you could call ghostly. The first two times you visit, you will see things that defy explanation: a flash of light on the side of the road, a strange noise, perhaps the sound of something brushing against your vehicle, the music on your radio turning to static… These things happen to all of us on occasion, but when you're on Weary Road, something out of the ordinary always happens. A couple local teens said they "never drive on Weary Road at night—especially in the summer. It's just too creepy."

One possible location for haunting of Weary Road.

The third time you visit Weary Road, especially if you get out of the car, you might find yourself face to face with a man who vanishes into thin air. Some say it's the ghost of Old Man Weary, some say it's the young man who died car surfing. Whoever the ghost is, it's usually enough to scare you back into your car and away from Weary Road.

I spoke to several people in Evansville. A couple in their 40s said they never heard the Weary Road story. A group of teens at a gas station, however, said the Weary Road ghost is a legend not only in Evansville, but the surrounding towns. Each had differing ideas of what part of Weary Road is supposed to be haunted.

I drove down Weary Road during the day. In some places it was clear, some places foggy. I didn't see a phantom vehicle or experience anything out of the ordinary, but Weary Road does give off unsettling vibes that are hard to shake even once you're far away.

They Talk To Dead People

Wonewoc Spiritualist Camp, Wonewoc.

Perched on a hill overlooking the quiet town of Wonewoc is the Wonewoc Spiritualist Camp, an auxiliary of the National Spiritualist Association of Churches (NSAC). The camp is where readers talk to dead people on a regular basis. The Wonewoc Spiritualist Camp began in 1874 and was incorporated in 1901. The original members of the camp came from Lily Dale, New York.

"We don't try to convert or convince. We embrace all religions," says Judith Ulch, reader and researcher at the camp.

The camp consists of thirty-seven acres, thirty-six historic cabins, gift shop, and six-unit motel. I recently spoke to Ulch at the Spiritualist Camp, northwest of Madison. The camp is a community. The cabins here are homey and small; some are one room, some are two to three rooms, all built in the 1930s and 1940s. The reason

for the difference in size; it all depended on how much money the mediums had to spend on their cabins. Today, the camp owns the property the cabins sit on, and they always will. It is in a trust and will always and forever be part of the NSAC.

What makes Spiritualists unique (besides the fact they see people who are no longer considered living) is that they don't believe in hell or sin. They believe we never die, and say this has been proven scientifically.

The grounds at the camp have healing qualities. The spiritual nature of the camp has been revealed in a photo. A huge ball of light was photographed in the cabin next door to the post office at camp.

Energy from all the psychics stays here, so this is one reason the grounds are so different than anywhere else. If you check out the Spiritualist Camp to see what they offer, you might be surprised at the variety: meditation, table tipping, workshops, and readings. The readers keep half of the modest fee they charge for their services; they do not tell fortunes, they perform readings.

Some of the camp's many historic cabins.

Priscilla and Patricia Ralls beneath the Healing Tree.

Friday nights at the Spiritualist Camp are circle nights. But don't let the name put you off; none of the psychics go into trances. They could; they just don't want to.

Also a big draw on the grounds: The Healing Tree, which is said to have healing powers.

Hilda First is the current president. She once was a reader, but no longer does readings because of health issues. Acting vice president is Soniya Davis.

Judith Ulch

Ulch believes everyone has the ability to see those that have passed in a physical sense. She also believes some people are naturals. She says, "Developing your spirituality is one way to open yourself to new experiences."

Ulch sees spirits all the time. "Earthbound spirits don't know they're dead." The spirits she sees have crossed over and are there most often to speak to relatives.

Ulch has had many first and secondhand experiences of a spiritual nature. She told me that her mother had a spirit around

her that she used to see when she cooked. When a woman gifted in reading and automatic drawing came to her mother's house, she drew a picture of a young girl with a huge belly. She told Ulch's mother that the young girl, from the 1700s era, was traveling through the area and stopped near a lean-to while her husband went to hunt for food. Unbeknownst to each other, the husband was killed when he was hunting and the young girl died giving birth. These two spirits are examples of earthbound spirits because they don't know they're dead. When the reader showed Ulch's mother the picture she had drawn, Ulch's mother was stunned—it was the girl she had been seeing around her when she was cooking.

The ability to see those that are no longer living among us is a gift that others in Ulch's family possess as well. When Ulch's father passed away, her son, Jason, knew it without being told. He saw his grandfather standing near his bed that morning and later called Ulch to say "Grandpa died."

Spirits are not always passive. Jason's grandpa even saved his life one time. Jason was driving his motorcycle when he flew off a curve and down a stony bluff. The entire side of the bluff was jagged rocks and completely hard, with the exception of one small grassy area. Jason said he felt his grandfather pick him up and put him down on the grassy spot. Anywhere else and he would have died. Jason told his mother that he felt his grandfather's presence so strongly that he not only saw him, he smelled him.

People come to the Wonewoc Spiritualist Camp to get insights and answers. When Ulch gives a reading and feels her brother's touch on her shoulder, she knows a suicide is attached to the person receiving the reading, because her brother committed suicide. Rather than being sad, Ulch says her brother is happy now. He even "talks" to his family now, though he didn't for four years following his suicide. Ulch says suicide victims want the rest of us to know they are not mentally ill or crazy—they just can't live here. When Ulch sees her brother, she sees him as he was when he was about twenty-five years old; this is younger than when he died.

Ulch's brother visited their sister on her birthday with a dozen roses and wished her a happy birthday. Ulch's sister said she could see their dead brother so clearly, it was if he was in the room with her. It just so happened that she was in bathroom at the time. The sight of her brother startled her so much, she said she was glad

she was sitting down, otherwise she might have fallen down! When she asked their brother where he was for the four years after he left this world, he told her that while he had "things to say" now, he just didn't want to say anything up to that point. The best part of the visit: He said he was okay and not in pain.

This is a recurring theme that is certain to comfort the loved ones that death has left behind. Ulch says when people are dying from diseases that are long and hard, they experience pure joy just before they die and are pain free in their last seconds. Ulch says that spirits often encourage loved ones to refrain from drinking (alcohol).

Ulch was a young girl when she became aware she could see those who had passed away. She didn't really think too much about it because she had been raised by people who could see those who had passed away. She says her grandmother, a tiny woman, planted things by the light of the moon and was involved in natural healing, the kind of natural healing performed by the Native Americans.

Ulch distinctly remembers the very first time she saw someone who had passed away. She was about eight, sick with tonsillitis, and was in bed. At the time, she thought she was going to die. She remembers seeing a "Jesus" person standing at the end of her bed, though she knows he wasn't Jesus. He told her, "You're going to be okay," and put his hands on his own throat. Not long after, Ulch recovered.

Ulch believes people are still very resistant to the idea of someone having the gift of seeing and being able to read and heal. When she was young, she couldn't tell the kids at school about her talents; now that she's an adult, some have trouble accepting what she does.

"At night at camp, I've seen people walking by in long dresses, even after camp is closed and I'm by myself," said Ulch. One time she saw a man in 1800s or early 1900s dress wearing what looked like a bowler hat, which he tipped as he passed by. She realized it was Andrew Jackson Davis. Davis wanted to get children involved in their religion, because without children, a religion will die.

She also said when they hold services, they've heard children laughing and playing, yet there were no children on the grounds. "The good stuff that happens at camp stays here," she says.

With a smile, Ulch remembers when she was little. She and her cousins would kiss their grandma on the face when she pretended to sleep. Her eyelids would flutter and they would kiss her cheek. When she kissed them back, they would giggle. When Ulch's

grandmother passed away, she went to the casket and says she saw her grandmother's eyelids flutter. She started to laugh because that's what her grandmother did when she was alive. Thinking she was crying, her cousin went to her. Ulch told him the reason she was laughing and soon they were both remembering and laughing. Ulch says this was the best funeral she ever went to.

The interview with Ulch was an intensely personal rexperience for me. On the way to the Spiritualist Camp, my two friends, Priscilla and Patricia Ralls, and I were discussing whether we had ever had a "ghostly" experience. Priscilla said she often thought of her mother, but didn't feel her presence in a physical sense. Patricia, avidly interested in the spiritual and religious realm, couldn't put her finger on any one thing that would qualify as an experience or encounter. I mentioned to them, as I have to my daughter and mother, that I feel my grandmother's (my mother's mother) presence very strongly. Though I've never "seen" her, I feel a connection. We talked a little more, and forgot all about it—until about an hour later.

Because camp was closed, Ulch couldn't give a reading, but she did say she saw my grandmother on my mother's side (my exact words to my friends) standing next to me. Ulch couldn't see what she looked like, but told me a number of things specific to my situation. While Ulch was telling me what she "saw," I was overwhelmed by emotion. To this day, I have never felt anything like it. I plan to return with others to get a detailed reading when the camp is open for the season again.

Soniya Davis

Soniya Davis started out at the camp by volunteering part-time. Now she's the acting vice president. She's originally from the Chicago area, but moved to central Wisconsin nearly thirty years ago. She believes her health and well-being are due largely to the Spiritualist Camp.

She's no stranger to the supernatural. She remembers her mother getting tea leaves read and seeing a medium.

The last decade has been rough for Davis. Her mother passed away in 1998, and her husband passed in 2002. Davis was in bad shape. She suddenly had two houses she couldn't afford because health problems prevented her from making a living. Despite this preponderance of trouble, she still received "messages" from those she loved that had passed from this earth.

Her husband was a WWII vet and had always watched nonfiction on TV. Davis remembers one particular evening, shortly after her husband had died, when she was in so much pain that she was sobbing. She unknowingly had the TV on the Sci-Fi Channel and John Edward was talking. Suddenly, she smelled Polo™ cologne, the scent her husband used to wear. Davis then looked at the TV and realized what and who she had on. She then said, "Oh my God, Donald, do you want to talk to me through someone like John Edward? If you do, then you have to give me a big, physical sign, because you know I don't remember my dreams."

She might not have gotten an immediate sign, but she certainly got one the next morning. Her computer was on in her bedroom while she was folding clothes. Davis says her computer was old and had a monochrome screen; no color—just black and white. She remembers walking out of the room and seeing the screen explode in color: orange, purple, red, yellow, blue, and green.

Though Davis didn't do anything then, she definitely regarded this explosion of color as a sign. Two years later, her friend, Sharon, called and asked if she wanted to go to "Spook Hill" with her. Spook Hill is what the locals call Wonewoc Spiritualist Camp.

Davis went and had her reading done by Katy while she was at Wonewoc. "Holy buckets! It knocked my socks off," she recalls. She was told so many things no one else could have possibly known.

In early 2006, Davis and her friend, Sharon, went to church at Wonewoc. Judith Ulch was holding the service. Ulch had one opening for a reading at 4:00 that day, so Davis drove Sharon back home and returned for a reading—that's how strongly Davis felt about having a reading done with Judith that day.

"For years, I blamed myself for not being near Don when he passed away," Davis says. Don was in the hospital bed and his sisters were crowded around her to help ease her sorrow. Davis wasn't able to reach him as he passed. She does recall his final moments, though.

"His eyes were goofy and he was reaching out with his left hand. I thought he was reaching for me," she remembers. When Ulch gave Davis her reading at 4:00, it was a revelation more than anything. Ulch saw Davis' husband in bed reaching out—just as he did when he died. Ulch imitated the way Davis' husband's hand and arm were positioned—exactly. Ulch told Davis that her husband was reaching out to his father to help him cross, not to her.

Davis was astounded by the number of personal revelations Ulch told her that ultimately helped bring a measure of peace to her that she hadn't had until then.

In fact, Davis was so impressed with all that Wonewoc has to offer that she asked if she could volunteer at the camp. She worked part-time in the office for a number of years; now she's the acting vice president.

"There's something special about her," Davis says of Ulch. Davis attributes Ulch with literally saving her life by helping her beat her addiction to prescription drugs and helping her to understand all of her past life.

Davis has had a number of other encounters with the dead. She remembers getting a whiff of her mother's perfume. Davis and her mother shared an incredibly close bond in life. The bond has seemingly transcended physical death.

At one of the lowest points in her life, when she was desperate to sell either of the two homes she had been saddled with, Davis went to the cemetery. "Mom, you gotta help me sell your house," she said. Her mother heard her; in four days, her mother's house sold.

Davis' marriage, like most others, wasn't all light and happiness. She remembers an argument she and her husband were having. Wanting it to stop, she held her parents' wedding picture to her chest and pleaded, "Daddy, daddy, please help me!" (Her father passed away twenty-five years earlier.)

A hurricane lamp in between the living room and kitchen suddenly lifted up and tumbled to the carpet in slow motion. However, when it hit the ground, the glass didn't break. Davis' husband, who had witnessed the episode, immediately went to bed, ending the argument.

Another particularly striking event that made an indelible mark on her was when she says her mother paid her a visit. Davis layed down to rest, not asleep, but more like in a trance. She remembers going into her spare bedroom where the room was completely pitch black and opening a dresser drawer, franticly looking for her checkbook. Instead, she found a picture of the man she had recently reconnected with, whom she had been engaged to forty years prior to her marriage to Davis. She says the picture was in a bright golden light while everything else remained in total darkness. Then she says she heard her mother talking to her cat in the living room just outside the spare bedroom. When Davis went into the living room, the house was in bright sunlight. As her mother stood standing silently smiling, her mother dropped her cigarette

case onto the coffee table (the case tumbled in slow motion). Davis says she then went to her mom and hugged her very tightly and said over and over again, "Oh mom, I miss you; I love you so very much." As Davis held her mom, she remembers saying to herself, "You've got to wake up so she can hear you. You've just got to wake up so she can hear you." Of course, when Davis opened her eyes she was lying in bed, and her mother was nowhere to be seen. Davis firmly believes that this was a visitation from her mother, giving her the message that her long lost love was going to be the one to help her start a new life. Davis also believes that her mother was actually responsible for reconnecting them for that purpose.

Davis said when her mother was alive, they were like one person. Their bond was so strong, it was more than mother and daughter, more than sisters; it was like they were twins. Davis has discovered, through Spiritualism, that there are twin souls. So, according to Spiritualism, the feeling she has had since childhood appears to be a twin reality. Davis was holding her mother's hand when she passed. Her mother still honors this incredible bond. Twice, Davis has asked her mother to see her; twice her mother has come to her.

Davis' husband didn't share her thoughts about communicating with the dead when he was alive and well. He used to say, "When you're dead, you're dead." His view changed when he found out he had lung cancer, and it was too late to do anything about it. Davis will never forget what he said to her shortly before he died. "I guess I'm going home," he told her. When Davis went to the funeral home to make arrangements, she only looked at one casket and selected it because it had inscribed on the inside "going home." Was this a coincidence? Davis says that she now realizes there are no coincidences in life.

After her husband passed, a different reader at Wonewoc gave Davis a message from her husband: "I'm sorry life wasn't different." The reader told Davis that her husband wanted her know that he appreciated all she did for him.

Davis believes her husband is "working through things on the other side." She says it's important to remember life is only a temporary place, and we choose what lessons we want and/or need to learn when we come back.

Learn more about the Wonewoc Spiritualist Camp at: audiomartini.com, nsac.org, and campwonewoc.com/index.html. A visit there may change your life.

Cave of the Mounds

Cave of the Mounds is named after the Blue Mounds, two large hills that are one of Wisconsin's most identifiable landmark features. The West Mound is 1,716 feet high, making it the highest point in southern Wisconsin; the East Mound reaches 1,489 feet. The world-famous Cave of the Mounds lies under the south slope of the East Mound. More than 100,000 people visit Cave of the Mounds each year.

Cave of the Mounds is a place that is mentioned as being haunted, but no one seems to know just who is haunting the cave area, or if the ghost is seen above or below ground. Cave of the Mounds was only recently discovered because it was sealed off. It wasn't until blasting took place in the area that the wonders contained below the earth's surface were revealed.

Some speculation is that after the blasting occurred, in the interim between when the discovery was made and when it was opened to the public almost seventy years ago, someone or perhaps *someones* may have died down there.

Another suggestion is that the cave complex was inhabited by Native Americans in the area and it is they who haunt the region below the mounds. A final suggestion, and one that makes sense, is that the ghost, or ghosts, who inhabit the cave area are actually the original owners or descendents of the owner, Ebenezer Brigham, who settled in the area in the early 1800s.

No matter what unearthly being dwells below the surface of the earth, it would seem they are definitely not warm-blooded. No matter the temperature outside the cave, the internal temperature seventy feet below the surface remains a cool and constant fifty degrees Fahrenheit. Add that to the 100 percent humidity and you've got a recipe for comfort when it's thirty degrees below zero Fahrenheit outside the cave.

I've been to the Cave of the Mounds, and I still remember the odd feeling I got in a couple different sections of the cave, and I'm not claustrophobic or easily creeped out.

Some visitors get the feeling they are being watched—sort of like the watcher ghost story, only inside the earth. Others see shadows flitting where there should not be shadows.

The interior of the caves are not the only place people get the feeling they are not alone. This feeling continues for some, even when they are on solid ground outside the cave, walking on a trail or the park grounds.

Cave of the Mounds was designated a National Natural Landmark in 1988 by the United States Department of the Interior and the National Park Service. One of Wisconsin's most famous attractions, Cave of the Mounds is located at 2975 Cave of the Mounds Road, Blue Mounds, Wisconsin 53517. You can find out more about Cave of the Mounds by calling (608) 437-3038, or by visiting caveofthemounds.com.

Blue Mounds

O nce known as West Blue Mounds, then Pokerville, Blue Mounds was once a bustling lead mining town. The original vanished village is Dane County's earliest town, but Blue Mounds has another claim to fame—ghosts.

As you might imagine, the name Pokerville got its name from the rollicking nightlife that was once an integral part of the mining town. It's impossible to know how many people died in gambling disputes, drunken arguments, or other acts of violence that occurred in the city or along the infamous Ridgeway Route, but it's likely that at least some of the ghosts said to haunt Blue Mounds are a result of those wild times.

The Watcher

The watcher is most often a benevolent ghost associated with a soldier or some type of ghost, whose duty it was to stand guard or watch—hence the name watcher. The watcher ghost stems from the Blackhawk War time period. These ghosts are not aggressive. They are passive and thought to be more likely sentinels.

The interesting thing is that whole families in the area have seen the Blue Mounds watcher for the past 150 years. The watcher has been seen in other nearby areas, too, though Blue Mounds is the spot the watcher is most likely to be seen.

Watchers can be seen on a bluff, a ridge, or even in a tree. They are said to have a lot of power over people—mentally. Instead of commanding someone to do something, they use their power to calm people. It's sometimes referred to as a form of hypnotism. In the old days, watchers used to hang around the mound and forts and towers.

The watcher is believed to have been many things: a guard left out on sentry duty, a cursed militia soldier, and even a spirit guide. No matter what the watcher was, these ghosts have been seen by hundreds (maybe thousands) of people in the Blue Mounds area.

The House On Hyslop Road

Dane, Wisconsin.

Madison area writer, Ruth Forrest Glenn, author of *Executor Takes All* and *I'll Take Care of You*, not only writes about otherworldly experiences, she experiences them, too. That might be because she's in tune with things that are off the radar as far as most others go. Or maybe because she's aware of the things around her that slip out of most people's consciousness without them being aware that they even missed anything.

Forrest Glenn remembers the old house she lived in some years ago. "I knew something was different about the old house," she says. It didn't take long for her to realize there was much more to the house than could be seen with the human eye.

Hyslop is a long and winding road, right after you turn off Kopp Road. The house she lived in, filled with the spirits of the no longer

living, is just past a large empty field, and close to a Christmas tree farm. The house was built in the 1870s and is fashioned from cobblestone. The only thing that has changed since it was originally built is the addition of a living room to the front of the house many years after the main building was erected.

The old part is where you can "feel" the spirits that still remain in the house. Forrest Glenn says, "The vibrations that could be felt standing in the old part rather than the new were earth-shaking."

She admits the time she lived in the house on Hyslop Road was when she was at an emotionally vulnerable point in her life. She was on her own and trying to overcome abuse she suffered as a child as well as other tragedies.

Some might call the house she lived in creepy. Not Forrest Glenn—she felt an immediate bond with the spirits in the house as well and the house itself. She remembers her first experience well. "I have a habit of having a cup or two of instant coffee late in the evening and before bed sometimes. It helps me keep up with the writing schedule I've adapted to. The water at this old house was from the well that had been there since the house's beginnings, over a hundred years." She says, "It was the cleanest sweetest tasting water I had ever drank, and I soon became addicted to it. I didn't really drink a lot of water over the years, but I couldn't seem to get enough of this water. Now I drink water all the time for good health reasons, but I'm sure I picked up that trait at the old place."

"Anyway, I placed my cup of water in the microwave and I always heated it for two minutes. It made the water really hot. I would let it sit for a few moments as I finished my writing or studying. Beside the microwave on the kitchen counter, I would set the small can of instant coffee with its plastic lid snapped shut, and lay a spoon out." She'd done this so many times it had almost become a ritual.

On this particular day, when she came back out of the bedroom to retrieve her coffee, her cup was sitting on the countertop, the microwave door was shut, the coffee can was open, and the lid was slightly placed over the can. Even more amazing—the coffee was already in her cup and it had been stirred with the spoon left in it! "It didn't scare me because I have always been open to whoever, whatever helps us get through this life." This experience just gave her more prospective into the things

that she believes cross our life path for some reason or other. "There were many strange things I felt and saw in the house," she says. "I felt a strong attachment to the spirits in the house, individually and as a whole. There was a strong pull of grief and differences in spirits, just as people's personalities are different here." And by here, she means the earthly realm.

Forrest Glenn believes in spiritual protection in our daily lives. She had a roommate at the house on Hyslop. "My girlfriend upstairs was alone at night whenever her guy was gone with the construction crew. He put the steel beams in buildings. I could see him each day in my devotions and still now as I tell you about it. He would be high up on a steel beam somewhere, and I would hold him, envision bright, clear white light encircling him to protect him and not let him fall. My girlfriend and I would crack a smile at one another in his near miss stories, but we truly believed he was being taken care of by spiritual means." But there were also spirits doing their own things at the house on Hyslop. Forrest Glenn says, "My girlfriend's cupboard doors in the kitchen would open and close so much at night that she asked me one night to listen for a few days so I could hear them, too." "I was always up late, not sleeping well, and usually had headphones on listening to music as I wrote. For a while I cut out the music in the headphones and had it on very low. I heard a door shut after midnight, and keep opening and shutting into the wee hours of morning. I knew that my girlfriend would be asleep, because she had to be up at 6 am for her job. As I continued to listen, I could hear the cupboard doors opening and shutting. Whatever was in the house, really bonded with me and my friend. I had always watched for signs, but this opened a portal of understanding for me, one that I carry to this day with me."

"I wasn't sure what was coming in my life next, but I was open and thankful to those who had lived and died before me that made their presence known to me in this sanctioned house," says Forrest Glenn. "I was part of something that only a supreme entity such as God could take away from me, but nothing another human being could cruelly take from me again."

Forrest Glenn also remembers something else. "My friend and I shared stories. I learned that she also knew that someone (not alive) would lay beside her at night when she was alone. We both

had this experience. She told me she would say to whomever it was, that they could stay and lay there, as long as they did her no harm. They didn't—and she could feel them there until dawn." Forrest Glenn feels that the presence next to each of them was as comforted as they were. "I wasn't so unnerved about this once I had more understanding," she says.

Her daughters met the biggest presence in the house, a boy named Ryan, before she did. Forrest Glenn believes he was the leader of any children who had died at the quaint old house. After he felt comfortable making himself known to the girls, he made his presence known to Forrest Glenn in the house as well as the yard.

She and her young adult daughters, eighteen and nineteen, enjoyed playing with her Psychic Circle game. "We would play in the back bedroom that my youngest daughter had stayed in, on an old round table bought at an estate sale. One night, the board with its answers and questions, spelled out the name "RYAN." I love history, and I remembered something in the house's abstract about a family that had lived there in the 1940s."

She learned a fire had trapped a young boy, six years old, killing him. "When I went through my paperwork, I read about a boy who had died in the house; his name was Ryan.

"I started to hear a child's voice often in the home. I was sure that Ryan and I had admiration for one another. Such a sad event took his life and I empathized with him. I could hear him run down the hallway to the older part of the house on a regular basis.

"I saw the shadow of him appear before midnight one night. It was the night that the moon shows a lady in it. My friend and I had been talking late before we each went into the house for the night."

She was in the kitchen making her coffee. She put the spoon down and picked up her cup to take a sip. As she turned around in the dimly lit room, she looked toward the hallway and then toward the bedrooms. That's when she saw him.

"His hair was sandy brown and swept over his forehead, draping his right eye. His clothes were tattered but still intact." As she remained still for a moment, he stood up straight and flipped the hair on his face back, exposing both eyes. While she sipped her coffee in silence, the little boy stayed where he was. The moment she put her cup down, Ryan disappeared.

"After that incredible night, he only appeared from time to time in a mirror and in candlelight," she says. The little boy became a peaceful interlude in whatever woes were around her.

A few months before Forrest Glenn decided to move from the old house, she heard laughter in the hallway—not just from one child, but from many. She could hear them running down the hallway, a door opening and slamming, then another opening and slamming.

She says she didn't put things together until she was lying outside on the east side of the house getting some sun. This was near the end of the summer. She says she didn't lay out alone in that particular spot very often, as it was a hill leading down into a ditch that separated the yard from the woods that surround it. On that particular day, however, she was in an introspective mood, and thinking about the little boy and the others that she had seen, heard, and felt in the house. As she lay there, she kept hearing children running and laughing.

There was a long hall closet between the two bedrooms in the oldest part of the house, that she hadn't paid too much attention to before she started packing her belongings for the move. As she began to clean the closet out, she realized that at one time it had been a back porch and enclosure. She had a dream that night, that children were running and laughing, closing the doors to go outside and play or do their chores. She is convinced that most of the house's hundred-year existence was a happy home for children. She also thinks that the other children whose presence she felt there had drawn Ryan's spirit closer to them in the afterlife to undo the terror of the fire and allow the boy to be at peace.

Forrest Glenn moved out a month later. She says she felt the house sigh as she and her friend were gone from it.

But otherworldly events happened outside the house, too. Forrest Glenn remembers driving home from work one day, discouraged. She was in tears and could barely see. Luckily there was no other traffic on the road besides herself.

"I turned the corner and wiped my eyes with my hands." What she saw next wasn't the sight she expected to see—the field on the left was illuminated almost in a shiny haze. As the car came to a stop, she took the palm of her left hand and said, "Okay God, what do You want from me? What can I do to help myself and those around me who are suffering? It's not like I can change anything with the wave of my hand."

As she said those words, she slowly raised her left palm. "In the left field I saw brightness and vapors in shapes come up from the ground. It was as if I had conjured up what I had asked the spiritual plane for. Wrapped in the moment, I raised my right palm as well and saw the same illumination in the field on my right that even blocked my view of the house itself in the distance."

"I felt much lighter in spirit that evening, but have never been able to forget the brightness of light in my tears, that I saw that particular moment. From that point on, I was never able to turn at that corner without remembering what I had seen there, and seeing it again in my mind's eye."

Forrest Glenn still goes out of her way to drive by the Hyslop house on her way to her current home. She remembers the spirits of the house with love and thanks.

House On Taft Street

The lady in this old two-story house on Taft Street doesn't want her name mentioned, so I'll call her "Barbara." She lives with her parents and they're getting on in age. She's afraid of what the publicity and possible "embarrassment" might do to them if ghost hunters started contacting and bothering them.

As an aside, Barbara says she believes three houses in a row on Taft are haunted. She's come to this conclusion because of what the neighbors have told her about strange occurrences in their homes. They've complained about doors slamming in front of them, faces appearing in mirrors and then immediately disappearing, and creaking footsteps that circle them when they are seated.

One neighbor sheepishly admitted that she can sometimes "feel someone gently nudging her along" when there's something she should attend to, like a pot boiling over on the stove or turning off a faucet.

Barbara said this neighbor doesn't feel threatened by the nudging ghost, but the other neighbors say the presences in their homes are not quite so friendly. The ghost in Barbara's house, she tells me, is a cross between good and bad—just like many living beings.

"The first time I realized there was something or someone in the house besides me and my parents was about a year ago. My brother and my dad went to the store, and me and my mom were watching TV. "Jeopardy" was on and we were guessing answers. For once, she was doing better than me. When she gave the answer—or should I say question—to something I knew she didn't know, I turned to look at her and she was sleeping!"

That would have been shock enough, but there was another old lady alongside her mother. The woman didn't look familiar. "I'd never seen her before, but I figured it was a neighbor or someone from Mom's church. I didn't know what to do, so I just stared."

Barbara says she felt an initial prickle of fear, but the woman with long gray hair didn't look threatening. "I opened my mouth to say something to her. I'm not sure what I was going to say, but it didn't matter. The old woman answered the next question on TV—*in my mom's voice.*"

Barbara said she jumped back. The old lady turned toward her. When Barbara screamed, the old lady disappeared.

The scream, of course, woke Barbara's mother and ended the day's friendly "Jeopardy" challenge. At first Barbara wasn't sure if she should tell her mother. She wasn't even sure what had happened. Finally, she told her about the old woman. Her mother asked for a description. When Barbara finished, her mother told her in a nonchalant voice that it was her great aunt, Maggie, who had lived in the house when Barbara was a child.

The fact that her mother was so nonchalant coupled with the idea that the house was haunted was almost too much for Barbara. "Does Dad know?" she asked her mother. Her mother said he knew about Maggie still being there, despite the fact that she was dead, but that didn't mean he had to like it—or her. Maggie, when she was alive, often let him know that she didn't care much for him, either. But as far as Barbara's mother was concerned, she always liked her mother's sister. Besides, Maggie often located things for her that were missing, and made sure that she was safe.

Barbara didn't know what to think. Her mother was old; and dementia ran in that side of the family. Maybe her mother was already starting to show signs. On the other hand, Barbara knew what she saw—a ghost! But the more Barbara thought about it, she realized there were things that had happened that she couldn't explain. She remembered losing things, then finding them right out in the open.

Most of all, Barbara remembers the comforting feeling she got on several occasions when bad things had happened to her. "I rarely shed a tear, but a couple times when things went really wrong, I'd allow myself a good cry. I'd stay in my room so no one else would know. In the middle of feeling sorry for myself, I'd feel a cool draft, yet I'd always have the feeling that everything was going to be all right. The weirdest thing: One time the cross that had been on the wall, ended up right alongside me. At the time, I thought maybe I moved it, but I know I wasn't that upset."

She says she tried to talk to her dad about the ghost in the house, but he said she was being as foolish as her mother when it came to ghosts. "There's no such things as ghosts! If there were, nobody would be able to move, there'd be so many of 'em around," he'd told her. She never asked her dad about ghosts again, though she and her mother discussed Maggie and other spiritual issues a number of times after that.

Barbara remembers another time when she was walking into the spare bedroom when she suddenly smelled baby powder. This was very odd as there hadn't been a baby in the house in decades. She quickly cleaned and dusted the room, continuing to smell the delicate, yet persistent, smell of powder. After she was finished, she found her mother.

"I asked her why she was wearing baby powder," Barbara says, even though she knew her mother didn't own any. "Even though I just knew Maggie had something to do with it."

"Oh, that's just Maggie," her mother told her. "She must be happy. She loved the smell of baby powder and used it until the day she died."

Barbara still gets whiffs of baby powder and other flowery scents every once in a while. Maggie never joined her or her mother in their friendly live games of "Jeopardy" after that fateful afternoon, but that's fine with Barbara. She's happy knowing her great aunt is around, and there for her if she needs her.

Lake Mendota

L ake Mendota and Eagle Heights bluff on the shore of Lake Mendota are said to be haunted by Native American spirits.

Horse Hill

There are three Indian burial mounds at the highest point on the Eagle Heights bluff on the shore of Lake Mendota that were made as long ago as a thousand years. All three mounds are visible from the walking trail that circle the top of Eagle Heights woods. Those who have walked through the mounds area say there is a definite spiritual presence, as if there is someone nearby watching you.

Horse Hill, known as She-heta-ka by the Winnebago, is the name for Eagle Heights. Native Americans believed this highest hill on the shore of the lake was inhabited by a spirit horse.

This spirit horse could be heard neighing and stamping its feet. Native Americans believed the spirit horse could be seen on cloudy or misty days on the top of the hill.

The Native Americans themselves were said to climb She-heta-ka to gain power from the spirit horse. They also went to the hill to fast and dream. No Native Americans have been seen on Horse Hill for many years.

Lake Ghosts and...Serpents

Sightings of phantom turn-of-the-century boaters rowing in the vicinity of the university have been reported by students and others. These boats and occupants appear to be engaged in a competition, and then disappear into thin air. They are usually only seen on days when the lake is very calm.

Another story with a supernatural bent focuses on something that may or may not be ghostly. A marine anomaly known locally as Bozho has been known to overturn canoes, chase sailboats, and terrorize swimmers. Many have reported seeing this serpent,

which some say resembles the Loch Ness Monster. If Bozho does exist, it follows that there might also be some former *Bozhos* (in the form of Ghohztos) who make their happy home in Lake Mendota, too.

Park House Apartments

When you first look at this completely renovated prairie-style apartment house, you might wonder if Frank Lloyd Wright had a hand in designing it. Or you might wonder if there's an apartment for rent. (It looks appealing; what can I say?)

But if you were to talk to former tenants, or stay for any length of time in one of the apartments, you might start tallying the ghosts there.

Just five minutes from the UW campus and downtown Madison, with rooftop views some would kill for (maybe the word kill is a little strong), the building doesn't immediately send out ghost vibes. Inside the building, however, is a different story.

Through the years stories have spread from renter to friend to family. Some stories are mild in nature; some make you wonder; some might even make you leave the light on at night, or just plain leave.

One renter I spoke to that lived there ten years ago remembers doors slamming for no reason and the feeling of someone breathing down her neck with icy-cold breath. Others who have stayed in the Park House Apartments have similar recollections.

The former renter who talked to me, however, remembers more than frigid breath on her neck. She remembers standing at the sink, washing dishes, and hearing footsteps walk right up behind her. When she turned around, there would be no one there. The first several times she thought it was only her imagination playing tricks on her.

The next time this happened, she heard the creaking of the floor as the footsteps approached. This time she spun around with a knife in her hand. The footsteps stopped immediately. In fact, they stopped abruptly as if waiting to see what she would do, only there was no one there. An icy blast of air whooshed over her.

Every time this happened, and it happened often, especially when she was at the sink, the footsteps would stop and a blast of air would nearly knock her down.

When she first moved into the building, she spent a lot of time looking out the window, daydreaming about the small town in

western Wisconsin that she'd come from. Then one day, she saw something other than a car driving by, or a squirrel on the lawn.

"I know I didn't imagine it," she says of the ghostly face in the window. "It was an elderly woman, and she would shake her head back and forth. To this day, I'm not sure what she was trying to say."

She probably wasn't happy, though. "She always had a scowl on her face."

This might have frightened many, but not this renter. "Sometimes when I got really homesick and was about to cry, I'd hear humming. It was really soft and really close to my ear. I know this sounds crazy, but it was like the ghost was trying to make me feel less lonely."

There were stories on campus that someone had committed suicide in her apartment, but she didn't investigate. "If I had found out that someone died in my apartment, I would have left immediately, lease or no lease. Sometimes, I think you're better off not knowing something really bad."

She didn't always get good vibes at the apartment; sometimes she got the distinct feeling she was treading on someone's toes. If she had friends or family over and someone got a little rambunctious, something would invariable come off a shelf and drop—heavily—to the floor. "These things would be against the wall and then slide off the shelf and hit the floor for no reason. The only time this would happen was if I was having fun. I never saw the face of the old woman in the window during those times, but I got the impression, she was still there, but interacting in a different way."

So who was this elderly lady ghost? The apartment building wasn't that old and the majority of renters when she was there were students.

The former renter also remembers her new TV turning on for no reason and doors opening and slamming shut. The scariest thing: She felt drawn to the window. "It sounds stupid now, but a couple of times I felt as if someone was willing me to go to the window and jump, and I wasn't stressed at the time." She says she was doing well in school, her family was healthy and happy, so she doesn't think it was her mind playing tricks on her.

She says she's heard stories about others who rented apartments on Park Street. The stories are similar: the chills, the door slamming, TVs turning on and off for no reason. She heard another story: A different apartment in the building was said to have a "haunted" closet.

She lives in Verona now but works in Madison. Every once in a while she drives by the apartment. She gets the same unsettling feeling when she looks at the window where she used to see the elderly woman's face.

The former renter said she never believed in ghosts until she lived at Park House Apartments. When she tries to come up with a logical explanation for what she saw, heard, and felt while she was a renter there, she says she can't. The only thing she can say for sure about what she experienced: "I had a roommate when I was in college. It just happened to be a ghost."

Ghostly Gorham Street Apartment

T he Gorham Street apartment C. J. shared with two friends was just one of several buildings—all on Gorham—that are reportedly haunted.

She said the house she lived in didn't look haunted on the outside, just old and rundown. When she lived there, she heard stories that two nice two-story houses a couple of houses down were also supposed to be haunted. "People talk when they wait for the bus," she says.

C. J. got her first hint that her apartment was haunted when things she would set out would move somewhere else on their own. She would empty groceries out of a bag, put them on the counter, and leave the room for a minute. When she returned, an item or items would be in a completely different area.

It really "freaked" her out the first time, although she tried to attribute it to thinking too hard about what was going on at school. When it happened several more times she "got a little scared." At first her two friends thought she was just being a "blonde," but then they started losing things. They decided to do a little experiment.

The three young women placed a half dozen apples on a cupboard in a straight line, made sure the door was locked, then went to watch TV in a different room. When they returned, the apples weren't even close to being in a row. And they were on a different counter!

C. J.'s friends were so frightened, they left the apartment screaming. They came back later, but C. J. remembers they all slept in a huddle that night in case the "ghost came back."

Then other things started happening. The girls would hear mumbling. The words were never distinct, but C. J. says they all got the impression that whoever was making the noise was disturbed about something. It almost sounded like someone was talking to him or herself.

Somehow, the three girls toughed it out until the end of the school year. C. J. says living with a ghost didn't kill her, but she doesn't want to do it again anytime soon.

Aztalan

"Hunted."

That's the feeling people get when they visit the park. Aztalan is called one of the most haunted places in the state. It's a place that is considered sacred—maybe that's why many get a feeling of unease here despite the beauty of the land and the lake.

Aztalan is one place that begs to be researched and visited. The State Historical Society puts out a lot of incredible information about cities, sites, and places all around Wisconsin. If you want to learn more about Aztalan, a National Landmark and also listed on the National Register of Historic Places, or many other places mentioned in this book, a good place to start is at the Wisconsin Historical Society Web site: www.wisconsinhistory.org. The society is located in Madison at 816 State Street. The University of Wisconsin Press also published a fantastic book, "Indian Mounds of Wisconsin," that delves into Aztalan and other fantastic sites.

But I digress. If you want to visit a place that is believed to be haunted exclusively by Native American spirits, this would be it. As I researched Aztalan, I learned a lot about the culture of the Native Americans who lived there. I also learned that, almost without exception, paranormal investigators who have investigated Aztalan describe it as "without a doubt haunted."

In case you don't know much about Aztalan, here's a quick location, history, and culture lesson. Aztalan is located northeast of Madison on County Trunk Highway Q. It's located on the Crawfish River, just south of modern day Aztalan. You may know that it's Wisconsin's premier archeological site, but you might not know that between 1000 and 1200 A.D., this Native American town was home to a large group of Mississippian people who had migrated from Cahokia, in southern Illinois. The site is fortified with huge timber and clay walls and features impressive earthen platform mounds.

Northeast of Aztalan is a line of conical mounds that mark ceremonial posts and the burial place of a young woman who appears

to have been a member of the Mississippian elite. No one is sure who this mystery woman was.

The young woman is one of the most intriguing aspects of Aztalan. Many believe she is responsible for the haunting of the area, but others disagree: Cannibalism was also a way of life at this site.

Yes, cannibalism. And maybe it had something to do with the fact that this once thriving community was suddenly and very mysteriously abandoned by the many who lived there. This is only one theory. There are others: Maybe the mysterious lady buried there had someone to do with it, or maybe there was strife caused by competition for trade routes or even the land itself. It was, after all, a prime agricultural and hunting site.

The entire Aztalan site consists of mounds. Among these mounds are places where groups of skeletons have been found. Many skeletons.

You can read all you want about the history of the site, but until you are there, you can't appreciate what is going on around you that your normal senses can't detect.

The land isn't the only thing said to be haunted, either. Divers that have been in Rock Lake have had strange things happen. More so when they are at the bottom of the lake in the area of the underwater pyramids.

Does this place get cooler by the minute, or what?

P.S. When you do visit, make sure you bring a good camera. Lots of really strange stuff has been captured on film.

Oak Hill Cemetery

Oak Hill Cemetery, Janesville.

Want to see white at night? Then go to the Oak Hill Cemetery at 1725 North Washington Street, home of 26,000 graves—but check the posted hours to make sure you aren't breaking the law.

There's a chance you'll see a lady in white, but there are other places in the cemetery where you'll have a good chance of seeing white strings of light, a lady in white, *and* white shapes.

The area by the Veteran's Memorial is believed to be a very haunted spot. Not only will you most likely witness the white lady in this area, this is the spot where many have recorded digital and voice anomalies.

Some have heard heart-stopping screams that seemed to originate right behind them and no one was there. Perhaps these are just the disgruntled sounds of those that have been reburied. Janesville's original burial grounds were located in Jefferson Park, but the bodies interred there were moved to Oak Hill Cemetery in 1851.

Oak Hill Cemetery is the largest cemetery in Rock County and was dedicated in 1851. Burials in this cemetery date from the late 1830s.

I visited this very large cemetery on a very foggy day in the middle of winter. Mt. Olivet Cemetery is right up against Oak Hill Cemetery and it's a little difficult to tell where one ends and one begins. But since I couldn't find any Mt. Olivet ghost sightings, but found and heard about a bunch of Oak Hill sightings, take the time to make sure you're in the right place.

Getting back to the fog... What I found a little unnerving, besides constant camera problems, was the fact the fog seemed to break up and move in shapes away

Hilltop markers.

from the main bank of fog. This was especially the case with one particular spot in the cemetery on the top of a hill. I kept wanting to look over my shoulder for some odd reason.

Old Towne Mall

Old Towne Mall, Janesville.

The Old Towne Mall, located at 20 South Main Street, Janesville, is believed to be haunted by a ghost who apparently has a compulsive streak when it comes to doors.

Not only does the ghost like to hold doors open, it also likes to shake and slam them. If it gets tired of the sound doors make, it will begin knocking and rattling the door handles.

Visitors to the mall have reported seeing shadows move just out of their line of vision. Apparently, the door slammer likes to keep his or her identity private.

In addition to door noises, other strange sounds such as a dog barking have been reported in the mall.

A merchant staying late one night says he heard the back door of his business shaking uncontrollably. When he went to investigate,

the front glass doors also began to shake. He could see through those doors; there was no one there. The ghost does have a gallant side, though. It's said to open doors for people. These people are usually shocked to see there's no one they can see doing the opening.

Another story of a door opening and closing on its own involves a student who was in a bathroom stall late at night; he had left a classroom to use the bathroom. When he was in the stall, he looked through a crack in the stall and watched the door open all the way, stay that way for a minute or so, then close slowly.

The door is a heavy wooden door. What's more, the clasp has to be pushed in before the door can be opened.

When I visited the mall, I didn't have any door opening or closing experiences. The mall was different than I imagined; it wasn't as "open" as a public mall. It appeared to be geared toward professional offices. It also had a "professional" smell, as if a dentist had an office there. I wanted to use a bathroom to encourage a "door" experience, but the bathroom I tried to enter had a sign on it saying it could only be used by businesses in the mall and their clients.

One mall customer said she's heard stories about the ghost but has never seen anything unusual happen at Old Towne.

State Capitol

Capitol dome, Madison.

Many think of the Capitol as the magnificent centerpiece of Madison, an architectural wonder, and a source of pride—and it is. It was also designated a National Historic Landmark in 2001, and if you ask me, it should have a place on the list of most haunted Madison area sites.

Most Madisonians know about the 1904 disaster in which the Capitol caught fire and burned. While no one died in this accident, the damage was so extensive that the state had no choice but to put up a new structure.

Few Madisonians know the story about the deadly disaster of November 8, 1883, in which many workers were injured or killed while extending the south wing of the Capitol.

What made the tragedy all the worse, was the fact that Madison didn't have a hospital at that time. The injured and dying had to be carried to the offices of the governor, insurance commissioner, and quartermaster general; some had to be taken to their homes.

The entire fourth floor of the south wing is believed to be haunted. This may be where the collapse began. Disembodied footsteps and doors that open on are their own have been witnessed by messenger staff.

Many other places inside the Capitol give visitors the feeling that they are being watched. Cold spots inside some of the upstairs rooms also add to the feeling that you are not alone.

Want to learn more about this magnificent building? Take the State of Wisconsin Capitol Tour at: www.wisconsin.gov/state/capfacts/tour_select.html. You'll be glad you did.

Capitol building entrance.

Walker House

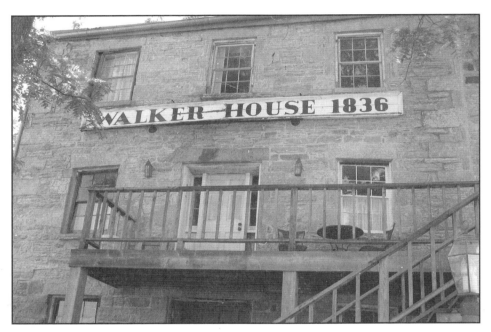

Walker House, Mineral Point.

This is one place that almost screams "Haunted!"

When I visited this old hotel, my first impression was that I was being watched. My daughter, who accompanied me, said the feeling that someone was watching her never stopped the entire time we were within viewing distance of the Walker House.

This old building fits in well with its surroundings. And not surprisingly, it's in close proximity to the tourist buildings, also said to be haunted, of Shake Rag Street. The Walker House has been the scene of numerous ghostly encounters and sightings that began well over a hundred years ago.

The building was closed for business when I visited it in late summer of 2007. It sported numerous signs that warned against

trespassing; one sign indicated that it would be opening in 2008. It didn't specify what it would open as or the exact date. I heard recently that the owners have experienced setbacks while renovating. At this point, no one is sure when the Walker House will reopen.

Let's start with the structure itself. It might seem surprising that this building, used as a bar, restaurant, and hotel throughout the many years it's been in existence, is in such solid shape. But maybe not. Many of the other old houses in this quaint town are still in great shape, too. Quality endures.

The Walker House ghost story begins in 1842, when a man named William Caffee shot and killed another man during an argument. Caffee's defiance and anger throughout his incarceration, trial, and the execution itself, remained constant—and high. His public hanging on November 1, 1842 at the Walker House was unlike anything I've read about. The condemned man was brought to the inn astride his coffin. Was he disturbed about his impending death? Well if he was, he had a weird way of showing it. He beat out the "Funeral March" with empty beer bottles on the way to the place where he would breathe his last earthly breath.

Area where hanging took place.

More than 5,000 spectators showed up to see Willie swing at the end of a rope.

The area around the building is heavily wooded, and said to be filled with invisible spirits. Perhaps this is Caffee and other patrons who frequented the bar in its heyday?

Caffee may be the only man who was hung on the premises, but former guests at the restaurant/hotel/bar, as well as employees, have seen floating heads and other apparitions inside and outside the building. Cold drafts are common. People have told of being locked in walk-in freezers.

Former Walker House workers recall doors slamming, doorknobs rattling, and doors swinging without the help of human hands. As if that wasn't enough—doors would lock and unlock by themselves. If someone put a key in a door lock, it wouldn't stay there for long. The locks would spit out the key.

If you think these are explainable things, how about pots rattling loudly and often in the kitchen—by themselves. These pot rattling tirades didn't involve one pot. Sometimes they rattled from opposite sides of the room; sometimes pots rattled simultaneously from each corner. Yikes!

In life, Caffee was said to have liked the ladies. In death, he's said to

have yanked girls' ponytails, snapped elastic (where he could find it), and tickled them—and not in a kindly, grandfatherly way.

Most disconcerting is the fact that Caffee isn't always an invisible ghost. He sometimes shows himself in various forms: young, old, as a cloud, and sometimes...a mutilated corpse.

Caffee's spirit is so strong that one man claimed he

Windows where strange things have been seen and filmed.

was transported back in time to see the very vivid hanging of William Caffee. I'm glad Caffee doesn't know how to use a camera phone.

The day I took photos of Walker House, there was no breeze, yet one curtain in one of the partially-open windows blew outward at irregular intervals. Was something unearthly responsible? Many have taken photos that show "evil faces" behind the glass. Some have seen faces appear in the window of the uninhabited building only to quickly disappear.

When the Walker House reopens, will Caffee be on hand to greet guests? Or will he bide his time before making himself known again?

After all, he's only been dead for a little over a hundred and fifty years. What's another year or ten?

Mineral Point Ghosts

Historic buildings of Mineral Point.

This town is teeming with ghosts. The old-timers there don't hesitate to tell you there are ghosts *everywhere*. They say most of the ghosts are remnants of the lead mining days and they are almost always rowdy.

Some of the more famous ghosts are victims of outhouse accidents. That's right, outhouse accidents. Long ago, the hillside boarding houses in Mineral Point had multistory outhouses attached to them. When I meandered my way through Mineral Point, I didn't see anything like that in existence today, but it isn't hard to picture such a thing given Mineral Point's many hills.

Despite the fact that nature quit calling long ago, the outhouse ghosts haven't. Stories have been told about moaning inside the ramshackle structures, and board-rattling—before the outhouses were finally taken out of use.

One specific story involves a former boarder who crashed through the rotten boards of the outhouse he was in and landed on a stone ledge on the bottom of the pit. This is where he died. Not a pretty picture. Maybe that's why this particular ghost kept hanging around. Not that he could change the chain of events.

If you're like me, this whole multi-story bathroom deal makes you wonder how things…well…worked. First of all, it wasn't as tricky as you might imagine. Even if the outhouse was a triple-decker, there were shoots off to the side of each separate unit. That's all you need to know, and hopefully all you want to know.

Historic Shake Rag, Mineral Point.

Another ghost of Mineral Point is the "Stable Boy Ghost" who was seen frequently years ago. Recent sightings have been sparse. This boy who was about twelve years old was once a regular at the lower end of High Street. He was also spotted alongside oh-so-haunted Highway 23. Those who saw him say he had a driving harness and horse collar slung over his shoulder.

The "Salesman Ghost" is one of the man "door-knocker" ghosts of Mineral Point. The Salesman Ghost usually makes his appearance after dark. He's been said to go from door to door trying to sell his potions like he did when he was alive.

The "Pastor's Ghost" has been seen sniffing the smells coming from local restaurants. He's believed to have been a circuit-riding clergy. While he seems to approve of the restaurants in the area, this ghost is not so approving of the local taverns. His face has been seen pressed against bar and tavern windows; and his expression is anything but happy.

Like many very haunted towns, the very earth itself is said to hold terrible secrets. Three Mineral Point streets are said to conceal subterranean chambers and tunnels, which hold the bodies of murder victims.

Long ago, South Street was home to a boarding house that had a secret passageway to a mine tunnel. The ghost of an organizer of the original railroad charter is said to moan in protest at his fate at one particular spot.

A Vine Street cellar chamber is said to house the ghost of a land speculator. Spectral moans coming from the area are said to be his way of saying he's angry he can't continue making money.

A hidden foundation on Henry Street is said to house the remains of a rival to the leaders of the early territorial government. But don't worry, he, like the others, just moans about his fate, nothing more.

A more visible ghost, the "Bounty Hunter," is believed to be an Englishman who was sent to Mineral Point to retrieve a Cornish fugitive. This ghost has been seen numerous times along Highway 151 between Commerce Street and Fair Street. Apparently, the poor fellow hasn't found what he's looking for. The Bounty Hunter is said to have died in a room he rented in a house on Ridge Street before he could accomplish his task.

Hobo ghosts are still said to haunt Mineral Point. These harmonica-playing ghosts can be heard near Liberty Street. And if you smell

stew—mulligan—it just might be a hobo ghost doing a little cooking. I drove past this area. It's beautiful to look at, but there is something about the place that gives you the feeling that while you're looking at it, something or someone is looking at you.

I visited Mineral Point years earlier to do research for another book. While visiting the Shake Rag historical buildings, I was told these buildings are haunted. Things get moved around, doors open and shut by themselves and sometimes these ghostly presences even touch visitors.

A friend's friend owns a hotel in Mineral Point that is haunted. The hotel owner and family had numerous experiences with cupboard doors opening, as well as mirrors and shower doors steaming up for no reason. I asked to use the name of the hotel and owner, but because they may sell someday, I was asked to refrain from mentioning either.

The ghosts associated with current day Mineral Point are those said to inhabit the woods opposite Pendarvis and the preserved homes of Shake Rag Street.

Human-sized shapes are regularly seen walking alongside the roads in the area, as well as in and out of the woods. Witnesses have even seen men in miners' clothing walking ghostly donkeys.

Idle Hour Mansion

This mansion is located at, appropriately enough, 421 Mansion Drive in historic Monroe. The mansion, built in 1857 on the city's northwest limits, boasts seventeen rooms and is an incredible example of nineteenth-century architecture that has withstood six major wars, many panics, and numerous depressions.

The man responsible for building the mansion: Arabut Ludlow, a businessman formerly headquartered in Chicago, whose travels regularly took him through Monroe on his way to Madison. The mansion originally stood on 3,000 acres which he acquired by means of a land grant at fifty cents an acre.

In the years 1846 and 1847, Ludlow built the mansion as well as the first bank and general merchandise store in Monroe. Smart move on his part; in the 1840s, Monroe was an important trading and marketing center. Ludlow and his wife raised five children in this mansion.

Ludlow died in 1896, and his family boarded up the mansion. It remained that way until 1937, when Ludlow's granddaughter and her husband purchased the property and what remained of the farm property. It's now open for tours and has a restaurant and bar.

When most people think of this Civil War mansion, they usually associate it with the part it played as part of the Underground Railroad. However, others know it as a place where a ghost resides. This ghost is Mrs. Ludlow, or Lady Ludlow, as she is referred to today.

Visitors to the mansion have seen things flying through the air. Lights are said to flicker for no reason. Some say this is Lady Ludlow trying to get your attention.

The building has cold spots throughout that have nothing to do with air-conditioning. One room in the mansion is always cold. Lady Ludlow's old room on the second floor has a definite chill regardless if the heat is on or not.

Want to see Lady Ludlow? The place she's seen most often is walking down a hallway at the back of the mansion. Another favorite haunt of the former mistress of the mansion is "Widow's Walk" on the top of the building. Numerous witnesses have seen her ghost, or a walking shadow, there at night.

The mansion is well worth a visit, even if you aren't lucky enough to see a ghost.

Stoner House

Historic Madison, Inc. has a wonderful story about this incredible Italianate house located at 321 South Hamilton Street. A little trivia: The two-story wonder, built in the 1850s, is constructed in part, of local sandstone. The Stoner House is now a Madison Landmark and is also listed on the National Register of Historic Places.

The house was originally built for Henry and Janet Staines, a family of Scottish immigrants. Yes, Staines, not Stoner. Stoner came later. In 1865, a butcher and his wife, Robert and Christina Nichols, owned the house for a short time. Joseph J. and Harriet Stone bought the house in 1865, and lived there for two decades. Joseph Stoner published birds' eye views of cities all across the country. These are now important records of the history of our country in the nineteenth century.

The Stoners retired in 1884, and Joseph Stoner died in 1917. Thomas and Susan Regan were the next owners of the house, followed by Varley and Ellen Bond, who lived in the Stoner house from 1922 to the 1950s. Varley Bond, who died in 1950, managed several department stores in Madison.

The Bonds undertook significant renovations, but over the years, the house fell into disrepair. It stood vacant and deteriorating for over a decade.

This is when the term "haunted" became forever associated with the Stoner House. After Bond died, tenants in the Stoner house told stories of the house being haunted by a white-haired, one-armed apparition dressed in a black shawl and dark clothes. This description fit Varley Bond, who was said to have died of grief over his son's death. Varley Bond only had one arm.

Varley Bond died a well-know and well-liked man. His son, Walter Bond, lived a short life that surprised many when the facts of his "accidental" death were finally revealed.

Walter Bond was a graduate of the UW who married Mary Ann Suster of Illinois in November of 1942. He was serving as a first

lieutenant in the ordnance division of the Army at the time. He was sent to Paris, France, where he met and fell in love with a woman named Germane Pesant. It was a serious affair; he said he would return to Paris and marry her after the war. He even made her the beneficiary of his life insurance policy.

True to his word, after he was discharged from the service, he left his wife and young child and returned to Paris. Once there, he met a rival suitor, Victor Jean Armand Fortelle, at the door of Pesant's apartment. The two men fought and Bond was killed. The man who killed him was later acquitted of involuntary manslaughter.

The accident that led to Walter's death turned out to be no accident after all. Worse yet for Walter Bond's widow: A Madison court awarded Bond's French lover, Pesant, $7,000 of his insurance money, and Mary Ann Bond only $3,000.

One can only speculate how distraught Varley Bond was, not only over the death of his son, but the details surrounding his son's demise.

In 1983, Madison Newspapers, Inc. gave the Wisconsin Architects Foundation the Stoner house. The house was then moved to the corner of the block to make way for a condominium project. The house underwent major restoration. In 1984, the $200,000 historically and architecturally sensitive renovation was completed. The Wisconsin Architects Foundation has had its offices there ever since.

Ridgeway Ghosts

Ridgeway.

T he words "Ridgeway" and "ghosts" are often heard and seen together. I've heard stories about the Ridgeway ghost since I was young and always wanted to know more.

After visiting Ridgeway I came away with a lighter view of the town than when I entered it. This town really knows how to make lemonade out of what other towns would consider lemons. Not only did Ridgeway embrace their ghostly reputation—they even put a ghost on their water tower!

Ghost on town water tower.

The town itself is a blend of hometown charm, sharply sloping streets (giving you an incredible view of the ghostly water tower), and lush woods and farms farther out. The darker side of Ridgeway, which I'll get to later, lies outside of town—some of it in ruins. Nearby Route 151 is said to wind through Wisconsin's best-known ghost country.

The Ridgeway Phantom was first reported in the mid 1800s. It was named for the small crossroads town of Ridgeway. This phantom took many forms. Sometimes it was a headless man, an old woman, a ball of light, dogs, and other animals.

Usually the phantom appeared from nowhere and attacked people on the Ridge Road between Mineral Point and Blue Mounds. At one point, there were so many "attacks," no one would travel the road alone or without some kind of firearm or knife.

The ghosts were traced back to 1840 when two young men were murdered at McKillip's Saloon in Ridgeway. A group of locals burned

one young man to death in the fireplace; the other one froze to death while trying to escape from town.

The Ridgeway Ghost was even mentioned in an article in the *New York Times* dated December 7, 1902. At this point in history, stories about the phantom, haunted houses in and near Ridgeway, and werewolves, etc. numbered in the hundreds!

The story in the *New York Times* focused on another victim of the Ridgeway Ghost, John Lewis. This man was prosperous, courageous, and above reproach. The story says Lewis was cutting through a field after helping a neighbor with some butchering and was confronted by a menacing figure that appeared out of thin air. When Lewis tried to pass, the ghostly figure put its arms out so he couldn't pass. The next morning a neighbor found Lewis, semi-conscious, and saying he had been hurled into the air, crushed, and pounded. He died a few hours later, insisting he had been attacked by a supernatural being.

Some say the Ridgeway Phantom left town for good when the town burned down in 1910, but others say it is still out there, in the woods near Mineral Point. Why this phantom would move away is anyone's guess.

Recent accounts focus on different types of ghosts or phantoms and different locations. Military Ridge, a bike trail that runs from Verona to Dodgeville, is where ghosts are most often sighted. The ghost is usually said to be a black dog that hangs around the trail and follows people. (More about that later in this story!)

Other more recent stories focus on an old, abandoned, and very haunted farmhouse on Highway 18 on the south side of the road. About fifteen years ago, this farmhouse was gutted. The windows were intact and you could see inside where the interior appeared to have been razed by fire. The exterior was so fragile, it looked as if it could be pushed over by hand.

Witnesses have reported seeing lights on inside the farmhouse some nights—which should have been impossible. The house obviously didn't have any electricity. Other nights, the house would be black as pitch again. Not so strange as it might seem. The farmhouse was said to be the former home of one of the legendary Ridgeway ghosts.

Then the farmhouse collapsed. The ghost, who is said to reside in the farmhouse, is fond of bothering travelers—whatever that means. On the bright side: No one has been killed by the Ridgeway Ghost in more than a century.

Ridgeway—The Present

In addition to the cute ghost painted on the town's water tower, the "Ridgeway Ghost" is featured on the town's stationery as well as the sign outside the town hall.

The townspeople are friendly and helpful. I did, however, have one experience in town that I found a little unnerving. But that might be because I already knew the legends about spectral animals haunting the area. While I was trying to get photos of the water tower, a black dog would invariably appear. It wasn't threatening, but it gave me an uneasy feeling. Every time I drove down or up a steep street and stopped to get out, the dog would appear a few moments later. Hmmm...

Fulton Cemetery

Fulton Cemetery, Fulton.

S tories about this cemetery, located in south central Wisconsin, include strange occurrences, equipment failure, and loss of power. Fulton is only about five miles southwest of Edgerton.

The cemetery is just off West Caledonia Road, north of the Yahara River. Classic stone pillars flank the entrance; the words "FULTON CEMETERY" on a small iron plaque assure you you're in the right place.

In the daytime, the cemetery is actually quite pretty. It's a tranquil setting and nothing stands out as threatening. I did see mention of batteries going dead, etc., so I made sure I had

Strange monument.

Long road into cemetery.

Edge of cemetery is perched on a hill.

Broken headstone.

fresh batteries in my camera. I didn't expect anything out of the ordinary to happen, though. The place is just too beautiful.

I began walking through the cemetery and decided to take some pictures inside the gates. Immediately my camera began acting up.

There are some really different gravestones in the cemetery.

This cemetery will always stick out in my mind because of how quiet it was. It wasn't just silent. It was eerily silent. Another thing that was very different about this cemetery was the location of certain graves. Along the road leading out of the cemetery, a number of graves and markers are perched on the top of a drop-off, or at the very least, a very steep hill.

Want to check it out for yourself? When you're on County Road H driving north, you'll need to make a left turn just outside of town; make a right if you're driving south on H before you reach the tiny town of Fulton. One you're on West Caledonia Road, drive for about a mile. You'll see the cemetery on the left. The graves are set way back in the woods.

Come with your phones, etc. fully-charged, and have extra batteries on hand. The scenery in the cemetery is out of this world and the feeling you get there is one you will never forget. Even if you may want to.

Old Baraboo Inn

Old Baraboo Inn, Baraboo.

This old inn really puts the "boo" in Baraboo.

The restaurant and bar located at the bottom of a hill in beautiful Baraboo, doesn't immediately strike you as haunted. The deep exterior color and architecture are reminiscent of days gone by. It takes little imagination to picture it as it once was—a hotbed of community activity. It's located across from the site of the old Baraboo train depot; the city of Baraboo once was a railroad hub between Minneapolis and Chicago.

I've heard and read countless stories about the inn. It's said to be a really active site for ghostly activity. Stories about ghostly

sightings are numerous and have been reported by newspapers around Wisconsin.

Recent sightings include seeing the apparitions of a woman dressed as a saloon dancer. The more than 140-year-old former saloon and brothel is now a restaurant, but its wild past is more than likely responsible for the ghosts that guests and others see today.

The ghost or ghosts have caused dishware to fly off a rack, a broom to float across the kitchen, and doors to open and close by themselves. Perhaps one of the most frightening shenanigans is when an employee goes into the walk-in basement cooler. Sometimes the door will shut behind them and the light will go off.

The restaurant and bar opened in 2002 after being vacant for fourteen years. Maybe the ghostly presence doesn't like all the current activity…or the new décor…or maybe it just wants a little attention.

This entity doesn't just stay in the restaurant and bar. There are two apartments upstairs. One renter ended up sleeping at a friend's house and began searching for a new place to live after he heard a woman calling his name and eerie tapping on his door.

The first tenants moved out after hearing piano playing and people singing and laughing—when the bar wasn't open. These tenants also saw the female ghost dressed like a saloon dancer others have claimed to see.

The 1864 building is the site of a number of deaths. Three prostitutes, including one that customers call "Mary," along with two former owners, have died here.

Some who say they don't believe in ghosts see things at the bar that eventually make believers out of them. Employees have seen Mary behind the bar. Others have seen a 200-pound griddle move by itself and a picture fly off the wall.

Paranormal investigators have come to the Old Baraboo Inn. Though some findings were inconclusive, some readings showed anomalies that could signal paranormal activity.

The locals say the food and atmosphere are great—whether or not you have a ghostly encounter. "If you see Mary, it's just icing on the cake," said one local. You can't get a better recommendation than that.

Old Baraboo Inn is located at 135 Walnut Street in boo-tiful Baraboo.

Haunted Baraboo

Ringling Farm

Those born and raised in Baraboo and Sauk Counties have heard stories about the Ringling Farm and Ringling Mansion being haunted.

The ruins where the once impressive house stood are almost impossible to find now unless you enlist the aid of locals, but the spirits still linger.

Some have seen ghostly circus performers there; paranormal investigators visit the site because of the rumors of ghostly animals and sounds, and also to capture EVPs and anomalies on film.

The Ringling Farm is similar to the Delavan area in that circus performers and circus animals spent a lot of time in each location. Another similarity: The sound of trumpeting elephants has been heard at the Ringling Farm and at Delavan.

Circus World Museum, Baraboo.

More information about the circus can be found at the nearby Circus World Museum (only a couple of blocks away from the Old Baraboo Inn) which is open to the public.

Here you can learn about the workings of the circus as well as intriguing stories about circus performers and animals that have passed from the world of the living. Some had a none too gentle exit from this world.

Highway 12 Hitchhiker

This story varies from person to person. Some say they've seen a spooky hitchhiker on a stretch of road that they see later on down the road—which is impossible.

Others say the hitchhiker has a black beard and hair, and looks rumpled, like he's exhausted from searching "or something." This same hitchhiker has also been seen wearing a green jacket as well as a tan jacket.

Those that have heard the story say the ghostly hitchhiker goes about his business on the south side of town, others say the north.

Like many ghost stories, there are some that say they've never heard the story of the Highway 12 Hitchhiker.

Man Mound County Park

Listed on the National Register of Historic Places, Man Mound County Park might not be the first place you think of when you think of Bara-boo! but it's right up there.

The park, located on Man Mound Road, features a rare, man-shaped effigy mound. Some might come because of the picnic area and playground. Others come for the chance to experience a really strange feeling while in this area.

Do Native American spirits haunt this park? Some say an emphatic *yes*! There have also been reports of seeing ghostly Native Americans in historic dress in the park.

Ohio Tavern

The Ohio Tavern, Madison.

W hen you talk to owner, Terre Sims, a woman with a ready smile and passion for history, you realize she is the perfect person to own this historical and very haunted building. She is also co-founder of Ghost Researchers In Madison (GRIM), and eager to learn more about haunted sites in Madison and beyond.

When she was looking to buy the tavern back in 1993, it didn't take long to discover the Ohio Tavern would come with a little "extra." She was sitting at the bar and saw cupboard doors open by themselves. She, of course, asked the bartender what was going on. "That's just our ghost," was the bartender's nonchalant reply. Sims says this was after she had

Owner, Terre Sims, opening the bank vault.

already signed papers—not that it would have stopped her. She's been at the Ohio ever since.

This tavern features friendly locals and a relaxed, happy ambiance. When you walk into the tavern, you imagine this is what "Cheers" would be like in the real, unpretentious world. A support pole in the bar sports many old backstage passes, and there's a trapdoor between the bar and the upstairs that was once used by those upstairs when it was a speakeasy. The upstairs patrons would lower a bucket with money and a note asking for what they wanted in the way of liquor so they wouldn't have to come downstairs.

No one can be sure who actually haunts the bar, though some believe a fifty-year-old ghost is responsible. The hauntings in the bar have been going on for decades and have touched nearly all the regulars in one way or another. Some even call the ghost "Ollie." They believe he was a short man who liked Old Style beer, wore bib overalls and smoked. He seems to make more appearances in the fall and also in February.

Left to Right: Kimi Matz and Terre Sims.

The building, built of red brick in 1913, was originally called the "Martin Loftsgordon Building" and housed the Security State Bank. Ten years later, the bank moved. The building was then the Martin Loftsgordon's mortgage loan, real estate, and insurance office. The "Loftsgordon" name is still on the vault in the basement.

Loftsgordon and his wife lived upstairs. In 1933, the Ohio Tavern opened and became the third tavern in Madison to be licensed after the end of Prohibition. One of the most important pieces of history associated with the bar: In the 1940s, a man is said to have committed suicide by hanging himself in the apartment located above the bar, a fact Sims learned after she bought the bar. This may be one explanation for the ghostly presence. Since then, cupboards have been opening on their own, unexplained noises and footsteps and a general feeling of an unseen presence have been a part of the bar.

Kimi Matz, a bartender at the Ohio Tavern for more than a decade, has seen her share of ghostly activity, yet isn't afraid. She considers it more of a playful presence, nothing that makes your hair stand up. When strange things start happening, she knows the ghost is around. "Sometimes people will put their coats and sweaters in a certain place. The next time they turn around, they're in a different place."

One of the more recent examples of paranormal activity involves the second stool from the end of the bar. "Three or four months ago, I was wiping the bar and the stools, and went to clean the machines," says Matz. "All the stools were facing the same way—toward the bar." She says when she turned around, the second stool that had been facing the bar, like all the others, was turned around. During the same period of time, the exact same thing happened to the janitor. When he finished cleaning, the second stool from the end had turned around; the others all stayed facing the other way.

About this same time another strange event happened. Sims remembers she was doing some painting in the tavern and held up a mirror she was about to hang. She decided to ask the "ghost" if he had any preference as to where she should hang it. She moved it around to a couple different positions, asking, "Do you like it here…or here…or here?" The bar stool moved toward the initial spot she had indicated, then dramatically turned in a different direction, then turned away from her. It seems even ghosts have trouble making decisions.

Matz remembers an experience one of the other bartenders had. "She was setting up all kinds of fruit juices. When she turned around, not one bottle was standing!" If the ghost is one thing, it's unpredictable.

Sims has photos that have made paranormal investigators and the curious alike sit up and take notice. A mysterious 2003 fire produced very distinct shadow people in one photo she now has hanging in the tavern. When I looked at it, it produced a strong (negative) reaction. Photos taken in the building now often show anomalies, especially where paranormal activity has been observed in the past. Sometimes cameras go out of focus or don't work at all. I had trouble with my camera several times when I tried to capture something in the tavern.

An old bank vault downstairs and a storage room are other places odd noises have been heard. When Sims took me on a tour of the basement, I had an odd shiver down my spine, though I didn't see anything. In the vault area, a new delivery man, not knowing the Ohio's history, took three cases of liquor downstairs. He said when he walked through, it felt like someone was watching him.

Radios don't work properly there, either. A bright light was also observed in the basement level. Conversely, shadows have been seen moving in one direction in the basement, too.

Sims has also had a very personal experience in the building. "I was going to be moving out of the upstairs apartment in a month. I went into the vault to get some things when suddenly a bottle of vodka leaped off the shelf and flew straight toward me. It missed me and crashed to the floor at my feet. I called for Randy, who was downstairs. He didn't see it happen, but it was the only time the ghost ever did anything to scare me." Was the ghost angry she was moving?

The upstairs apartment Sims lived in with her husband until he died was also haunted. Sims says her husband didn't believe in ghosts—in the beginning. She says, "One time we were both in the apartment. We heard knocking on the door, so my husband went to answer it. There was no one there. Thinking whoever knocked on it had somehow made it downstairs, he quickly raced down the steps. No one was there, and the security locks were locked." There was no way anyone human could have knocked on their door.

Her husband eventually became a believer when they went to bed one night and awoke to open doors everywhere in the apartment, including the oven door, refrigerator door, cupboard doors…every door.

The ghost in the building likes variety. A couple of the blonde female bartenders have felt someone tugging on their hair when they go downstairs, and one of them saw a dark shadow race down the stairs. Though there's no smoking in the bar, the smell of cigar smoke can often be smelled by patrons.

Rodger Horge, aka the Captain, one of Ohio Tavern's regulars, has seen a number of things. One time he witnessed things on the shelf literally flying off and landing on the bar. Luckily, nothing broke. He's also used to the sound of the basement door opening and closing on its own.

When employees are downstairs in the basement, they've sometimes heard the upstairs back door open. When they go upstairs to check to see who has entered the building, they invariably find no one there and the door locked.

The basement door, even though there's a latch on it, will sometimes open and close. Speaking of latches, Mary, one of the

Randy Austin at one of the Ohio Tavern's pool tables.

Ohio's bartenders, has been in the bathroom, sitting on the toilet, when she'll look up at the latch and see it move up. Is she frightened? "Nah. The ghost is friendly and harmless," she says.

Even now, Sims will make coffee in the morning while setting up the bar, and cupboard doors will open behind her. Maybe that's the ghost's way of saying good morning. She will sometimes say, "Yeah, yeah. Good morning," just to let the ghost know she knows she's not alone.

Other paranormal activities reported at the Ohio include personal items moving from their original position and balls on the pool table moving on their own. Some have blamed the fan, but the fan doesn't blow on or over the table.

Randy Austin, is an Ohio Tavern employee with a very famous great-great-great-(maybe one more great) grandfather, Moses Austin. Think Austin, Texas. Moses Austin was once a Texas land baron, until he sold most of his land to another famous Texan, Sam Houston. But enough about Texas. Randy Austin has seen ghostly activity, too. "I was in the middle of playing pool with JW, when he racked the balls and then said he was going outside to have a cigarette." Austin went looking for JW a short while later, came back inside the bar, and saw that the corner ball had moved to the corner pocket. All the other balls had not moved even a fraction of an inch; the entire rack was intact with the exception of that one ball.

The pool table is a common place to witness paranormal activity. Balls often move on their own.

Just sitting in your chair and minding your own business is enough to garner you a little ghostly activity. People sometimes feel that someone is brushing past them or touching their shoulders or arms.

Sims remembers one time there was so much ghostly activity in the bar that she drew a glass of beer, placed it in front of an empty seat and scolded the ghost. "Cut it out and drink your beer," she told the invisible prankster. The activity stopped.

One early March morning in 2005, Sims and two employees, Steve and Wizard, were working in the basement of the building. The sound of very heavy footsteps walking across the bar startled them. Steve thought he must have left the door open and someone was upstairs. He raced upstairs to see who was up there, checked all rooms, but found no one in the bar anywhere. Steve returned to the basement, told Sims and Wizard that no one was in the bar and then

resumed working. About a half hour elapsed and the sound of heavy footsteps walking across the floor could once again be heard. This time Steve quietly crept upstairs, thinking he could surprise whoever was walking in the bar. Again he checked everywhere someone could possibly hide; again there was no one in the bar. He returned to the basement. This time when they heard footsteps walking across the bar floor again, Sims just shrugged and told the two men to wave and say "Hi!" to the ghost.

Come in and say hi to the ghost yourself. The Ohio Tavern is located at 224 Ohio Avenue in Madison.

House on South Broom Street

South Broom Street, Madison.

The many bedrooms in the huge house (now office) and its prime location made it an attractive rental place, especially for college students. While it may resemble many other college rental houses, it has something most other rentals don't have—a ghost.

So many have experienced something paranormal in the house, that it has been labeled haunted for decades. In fact, stories about the woman ghost of 10 South Broom have been circulating since the 1970s.

Some students, hearing about the ghost in the house, actually went out of their way to try to rent it, hoping to have a personal experience of their own.

One student said having a real ghostly encounter "beats my 4.0 average all to hell." This sentiment is shared by many, and not just students.

The woman ghost has been seen on the first and second floors. Some have seen her wearing a dress from the late 1800s; some aren't sure what she's wearing because the experience was so unnerving.

One young man who rented there years ago said he had just finished taking a shower and thought he heard one of his (male) roommates walking and talking outside the bathroom. He thought he'd scare him, so he flung the door open, leaped out of the bathroom without his towel and found himself face to face with a woman.

Needless to say, he was shocked. His shock grew from there. As the woman kept moving away from him, he could kind of see through her. It was then that he realized it was the ghost lady. He said he let out a yell (though his roommates called it a scream) and raced back into the bathroom.

He remembers thinking, *Wait a second! There's no such things as ghosts*. He ran, still naked, back to the stairs and looked down. Sure enough, the ghost woman was still there. But not for long. She vanished into thin air as he stared at her. He said the event shook him up so badly he was afraid to leave his room for the rest of the night.

This same renter often heard his own door slam when he happened to be looking right at it and it was closed.

A different tenant from the 1980s says he often heard doors slamming when they were closed and also saw the mysterious woman ghost. He admits to being "scared out of my gourd," but never moved when she was in the area. She always seemed to keep going about her business. What he finds interesting is that she wasn't like the stereotypical ghosts he'd read about that instantly vanished when spotted. The ghost woman would look right at him or through him, and keep going.

General stories about the house include cupboard doors suddenly opening on their own and doors of all types slamming and opening when they were locked in real life.

Former tenants wonder if the new owner or owners of the building have had any ghostly experiences, or if they stopped when the college students moved out.

This old house is located near the intersection of West Washington and South Broom Street. It now houses an office.

Hauge Log Church

This unique church, sometimes spelled "Haugey Lauge," sits in what some would call the middle of nowhere. But maybe that's a good thing; it's home to one spirit or many, depending upon who tells the story. It is located on Highway Z near Blue Mounds, in western Dane County, which is one of the most haunted areas in southern Wisconsin.

One story is that lightning struck the hapless church not once, but twice. One of these times, a woman was killed. This woman is said to be the solo haunter of the church. One of the things associated with the woman said to haunt the Hauge Log Church is a tree swing bearing the woman's name that swings without the aid of human hands, even when there is no wind.

Others, especially the locals, say the sound of a woman screaming can be heard on quiet evenings. The phantom sound of wood crashing against wood has also been heard on occasion. When in groups, some will say they hear a woman screaming quite distinctly; others say they hear nothing. Does this mean some are more in tune with what falls outside the realm of "normal," or does it mean the scream is something the listener is hearing because it is a sound that is expected to be heard?

The look of the building itself is nothing that will knock your socks off; it looks quite plain. The history of the church, on the other hand, just might knock your socks off.

In order to keep this church from turning into a memory, it has "friends" to make sure it continues to stand as a testament to the early days of Dane County. The Perry Hauge Log Church Preservation Association, Town of Perry Historic Preservation Commission, Dane County Conservation Fund Grant Program, and the Knowles-Nelson Stewardship Program have all gotten involved in one capacity or another to assure this treasure remains standing, ghosts and all.

The small cut log church (it's only twenty feet by twenty feet) was used by the Norwegian settlers until 1887. That's when they switched to a new and bigger church two miles away. Hauge Log sat by its

lonesome for about forty years, until it was restored by members of the Hauge Church congregation. They wisely formed a committee to maintain the church.

In 1966, the Perry Hauge Church Preservation Association was formed; it manages the church's maintenance as well as maintenance of the adjacent cemetery. The church was placed on the National Register of Historic Places in 1974.

Speaking of the cemetery...yes, you guessed it, it's said to be haunted, too. At least a dozen spirits are said to make their presence known by making the hair on the back of your neck stand on end and also by brushing past you with a cold blast of air.

No one is saying if the woman who was struck and killed by lighting is buried in the cemetery, but I'm guessing there's a pretty good chance she is.

The Town of Perry where the church is located, leaped into action in 2000, when property immediately north of the church was sold. Actually, they leaped a little later when the owner announced plans to build not only a house, but a large metal storage building, just fifty feet away.

Area residents, angry and strongly against the plan to build so close to the church, blocked the owner's plans. In 2001, the Town of Perry adopted a local historic preservation ordinance. This was, and still is, a big deal. Few rural townships in Wisconsin take such strong steps to preserve history. Included in the Historic District are the church, cemetery, and surrounding farmland. Way to go, Town of Perry! The ghosts are undoubtedly happy, too.

The Town of Perry took things one step further in 2002. They acquired the thirty acres that surround the Historic District. The Hauge Log will remain part of Wisconsin history, for a long, long time.

Next time you're in the area, check out the church and the cemetery. Picture the history and the events that made this church worth protecting. And if you listen very closely, you might just hear the plaintive cries of a woman said to roam the church and grounds, or feel the light brush of those buried in the cemetery that are checking *you* out.

Tracks Of Columbia County

A Trio Investigates

This story comes from P. D., a woman who had heard numerous stories over the years about the haunted railroad tracks of Columbia County, and wanted to see if they were based on truth.

"Enough of these tales were told by older folk from the area that they were wedged in my being in that spiritual goose-bumpy way," she recounts.

One Saturday or Sunday, she gathered her friend, Kathy, and her daughter, Reese, with the purpose of walking the train tracks for at least a mile or two. She says she's had other experiences with life outside the body, and wanted to walk the tracks to see if she could feel the multitude of spirits said to have passed through.

The experience was one she will never forget. Twice before, she and her friend, Kathy, had walked the tracks. Both times, they saw things she calls "weird to the human eye." "It was a cold day in March of 2005," she remembers. "The wind was so brisk it felt like it was cutting its way through every bone in my body."

They started their investigation near a small town. As they walked the first half-mile, they talked and laughed. She remembers looking at her daughter and telling her how she used to dress her in all those layers of snowsuits, etc. that all mothers do, and then mimicking how she would walk all bundled up. All three "got to laughing" for no particular reason.

P. D. says, "But for the next few minutes we were quiet and I began to think of all those stories, the three train wrecks that had taken place within the eighteenth on into the nineteenth centuries that I had studied for the love of history. This area was very lively and all of the three major train wrecks happened almost to the day of fifty years.

"In the quiet, we all focused on one switch that had been used in the 1880s. It wasn't used after that time, but the platform for the original switch is still there.

"I was the first to step down off the train tracks to stand on this switch, to see if I could feel something of the past. As I stood there on the switch, that cold March wind ceased to blow through our bones. My friend and my daughter were agape."

She says they stood there in shock. The wind had died down to nothing in one instant. They stood there for a few minutes to see what, if anything, would happen while we they were on the switch.

"As soon as we set our feet upon the railroad tracks, the cold wind started blowing again."

Wails And Whistles

The tracks of Columbia Country attract many investigators and curiosity-seekers. Some are drawn by stories of ghostly train wreck victims at the scene of accidents that took multiple lives.

Some people come to feel the phantom breeze of a ghost train passing by. Some come to hear the whistle of trains, scrapped long ago, as they stand near old crossings.

The Columbia Country train tracks are said to be haunted by those who died without knowing what happened. They wander the tracks looking for those they loved and lost. The sound of crying children is a sound many have reported hearing along these tracks.

Resurrection Cemetery

Resurrection Cemetery, Madison.

Some say this cemetery is not as picturesque as Forest Hill, but many say the city's "Catholic" cemetery is just as haunted.

Resurrection is the final resting place of many famous Madisonians. The layout of the cemetery is unique; there are many burial patterns inside the cemetery's boundaries that reflect the religion, country of birth, and even parish boundaries of the person buried there.

This cemetery has an incredible past. I'll start with the Greenbush Cemetery in the 1860s, because this is where the "Resurrection Story" actually begins. It was at this time that the Catholics spent $170 for just over eighteen acres to be used as a new cemetery because it was

obvious the Greenbush Cemetery was too small. The new cemetery, Calvary, was established next to Forest Hill Cemetery. During the ensuing years, families moved bodies from Greenbush to Cavalry to be with other family members being buried there. Of course, some couldn't afford to move the bodies of their loved ones to Cavalry. It wasn't long before Greenbush Cemetery became the "forgotten" cemetery and fell into disrepair.

By the year 1900, nearby Dead Lake Ridge, crowned with effigy mounds, had been almost completely destroyed by quarrying firms. Only a small portion of the ridge remains today.

A couple of years later, an effort was made to restore the cemetery, but that effort was abandoned in 1908. That's when the Catholics got permission to use the Greenbush Cemetery site for a hospital. All the remaining bodies were moved to Cavalry. Sadly, the bodies and coffins had deteriorated to the point that it was almost impossible to tell one body from another. These bodies, in their final resting place (hopefully) in Cavalry are indicated with a historical marker.

The Catholics continued to buy land; as Cavalry filled, a new cemetery was established on this land. In about 1923, Holy Cross was established. Thirty years later, Calvary and Holy Cross were merged into one cemetery: Resurrection. More land was purchased along Franklin Street. Resurrection has finished growing in its current location.

The cemetery is a beautiful, tranquil place. Shapes reportedly have been seen flitting from behind one huge old tree to another. Others have reported chills for no reason in the "old" section of the cemetery. Some cite the unrest of the bodies moved from their original resting spots. The destruction of the effigy mounds on Dead Lake Ridge is another reason some say the cemetery holds such strong unearthly feelings.

The day I visited Resurrection, I was struck by the rolling peacefulness of the land; yet unnerved by three crows that followed me around the cemetery. Even so, I couldn't help but notice some of the lovely markers.

Here's something you might not have known: Historic Madison will host tours of Forest Hill Cemetery or Resurrection Cemetery upon request. How cool is that?

Every year, usually two Sundays before Memorial Day, the public is invited to participate in a tour of one of the cemeteries. What makes this so unique is that each tour has a specific theme. That's right, no tour you take will be the same.

You can learn about the fascinating history of Resurrection Cemetery by visiting Historic Madison, Inc., http://www.historicmadison.org/.

Spaulding House

The Spaulding House, Janesville.

In 1870, Joseph and Lydia Spaulding built this impressive home not far from the where the interstate now passes by. Joseph Spaulding died in his beloved house on August 12, 1877, but he may not be the reason the house is said to be haunted. A very public murder committed about fifteen years before the home was built, that left a body on the Spaulding property, may also be a reason for the continuous otherworldly presence there.

The body of Andrew Alger was found in the woods of the Spaulding property on July 5, 1855. Andrew Alger, a sixty-year-old lumberman, had picked up a hitchhiker a couple of weeks earlier. The hitchhiker, David Mayberry, attacked Alger with a

hatchet. Alger tried to defend himself with the only weapon on him, a pocketknife, but was unsuccessful. The heartless killer slit Alger's throat, dragged the body into the woods and took a nap. Later, Mayberry took Alger's belongings, clothing, and his buggy and left the scene of the crime. Incredibly, Mayberry hinted to friends in Rockford about what he had done. He was brought back to Rock County to stand trial, all the while proclaiming his innocence.

Violence accompanied almost every stage of the trial. Mayberry was found guilty, but justice was swift in Rock County in those days. Mayberry was hung by the neck until dead by a mob immediately after the trial.

Employees of this very old, former antiques shop have reported a number of paranormal occurrences. So many in fact, that some have documented their experiences in a journal.

Customers have also reported seeing things that could only be described as paranormal in nature. One customer saw a woman dressed in 1800s clothing entering an upstairs room. Other customers have heard whispering their ears.

Employees that close up for the night are sometimes surprised when they turn back to look at the house after they leave the building. Lights they turned off are now on, lighting up the interior of the building.

Sensational 1800s murder took place near the house.

Others have reported smelling fresh baking bread coming from a room that used to be the kitchen, and the ladies room is always warm, thanks to invisible hands cranking up the heat.

The Spaulding House has long been a spot of interest to paranormal investigators. Disembodied voices have been heard issuing warnings. Others have heard just the opposite: voices that sound conversational, or friendly.

This restored 1870s brick home is located at 3941 Milton Avenue in Janesville. It is open year round. Call 608-755-4160.

Church Road Cemetery

Church Road Cemetery, Lewiston.

This cemetery, tucked into a nook in the middle of nowhere, is also known by another name: Saint Michael's Cemetery. As a matter of fact, Church Road Cemetery is the only thing that exists anymore along this dead end road.

Trust me, if you weren't looking for it, you would have a hard time finding it. I went there in the winter when many trees were bare and I still almost missed it. The directions I had were terrible. I drove past Wyocena looking for it, then

back to Portage again, and finally had to buy a map of southern Wisconsin just to locate it. People that I stopped and talk to were friendly and helpful, but no one had heard of Maas Road—my initial landmark.

Most of the graveyards have dates from the 1800s; the last burial looks to have taken place decades and decades ago.

A church, believed to have been built in the mid 1800s, once existed near the cemetery until the 1940s. It's no longer there, but there is a big empty space in front of the cemetery, which is perched on a slope. Despite it being winter, and despite the heavy snow, I was surprised to find many footprints leading to the cemetery. I didn't count headstones, but I would guess there are fewer than fifty altogether.

Stories of a little girl that can be seen hanging from a tree in the cemetery have only gained strength in the past years. It's said you can see the girl hanging from the tree *and* hear the rope creaking back and forth. That's certainly a little different type of haunting than you usually find in your typical cemetery.

Cemetery is located on a dead end road.

Small, secluded, and haunted.

This site has been investigated extensively. Like many other reportedly haunted sites, some say it is very haunted, some say it's just an old cemetery.

Whatever your decision, it's a nice drive. And the long walk up the hill to the cemetery will get your blood pumping even if the girl ghost doesn't show.

The cemetery itself is in a serene setting in the middle of woods, but that doesn't stop thrill seekers from coming here—especially during the Halloween season.

If you have the time and inclination, you can find this cemetery by taking Highway 16 west out of Portage. When you see County Road O (Cemetery Road), make a left turn again. Drive for a what seems like an eternity, but is only a few miles, and make a right turn on Church Road. Don't go alone. It's on a dead end road.

Forest Hill Cemetery

Forest Hill Cemetery, Madison.

This incredibly beautiful and haunted cemetery located on Regent Street and Speedway Drive is considered Madison's most haunted cemetery.

Established in 1858 (some say 1857), Forest Hill Cemetery is the final resting place of many of Wisconsin's most prominent citizens, including eight governors.

An effigy mound group that consists of a goose, most of it anyway, two panthers, and a linear mound, are also part of the grounds. The head of the bird effigy was removed in the nineteenth century when a railroad was built through the area.

There's even a wooden marker in the cemetery, dating back to the beginning of the cemetery's existence. This type of marker was common then; the poor couldn't afford more permanent markers. Though no one can be sure who is buried there because there are no records, the body is believed to be that of Millie Kearns.

The "unknown" factor is widespread in this cemetery. There are 339 unknown Madisonians listed in cemetery records. Most of these bodies were buried in the village cemetery before they were moved here. (See Orton Park story.)

One man who is buried at the cemetery is the reputed son of Thomas Jefferson. Yes, *the* Thomas Jefferson. Easton Hemings, who lived from 1808-1856, moved to Madison from Ohio in 1852 with his wife and three children. He added the name Jefferson when he moved here.

Easton Hemings Jefferson was a cabinet-maker and musician. Other than that, not much is known about his life because he died shortly after arriving in the city. Much more is known about his two sons; his daughter, Anna, died young.

Easton Hemings Jefferson's oldest son, John W. Jefferson was a proprietor of Madison's American House in the 1850s. The establishment was just across the street from the Capitol. He led Wisconsin's 8th Infantry during the Civil War. Colonel Jefferson was mustered out in 1864, after he was wounded twice.

Much more is known about the youngest son, Beverly. He worked for his brother, John, served briefly in the war in the 1st Wisconsin Infantry, and also was a proprietor of the American House, later the Capitol House. He ran a carriage and trucking service and became acquainted with, and was well-liked by, most of the state's political leaders of the time.

Another very cool marker in the cemetery is the pillow on top of the Herrick-Doyon stone; it's supposed to signify "rest in peace."

Other sections of the cemetery are rather bare with few visible headstones. One-hundred forty-four unknowns are said to lie in Section 26; fifty-five in Section 33; and forty-eight in Section 32. Forest Hill has two Potter's Fields. Many have said these areas produce really strong feelings of unease.

When driving down the winding roads of this very large cemetery, you are struck by the different sections, monuments, and stones. Flowers soften the feel of this cemetery, but it is still a cemetery. I had a very strange feeling in the pit of my stomach near one of the areas

where there are few markers. Some get instant headaches near the military burial plots for Union and Confederate soldiers.

In a time long before Forest Hill was a cemetery, Native Americans used this high ground as a burial ground. Warriors are

buried in an effigy mound grouping, shaped like a goose on the southeast side of the cemetery.

Have a little time to kill? You can pick up a brochure for a self-guided walking tour of Forest Hill Cemetery from the office. The

entire cemetery is filled with a sense of history and reminders of the families who played a significant role in the area's development. A brochure, free of charge, that features a map and self-guided walking tour, or a publication by Historic Madison, Inc. entitled "Forest Hill Cemetery; A Biographical Guide to the Ordinary and the Famous Who Shaped Madison and the World" can (for a fee) be obtained at the Cemetery Office or the Parks Office. Forest Hill Cemetery is one of the first U.S. National Cemeteries in Wisconsin and is listed in the National Register of Historic Places.

With all the history buried in the cemetery, it's impossible to know how many different people haunt it.

Beautiful old monuments.

Memorial Community Hospital

Ask someone who works at the hospital if Memorial is haunted and they will most likely say they've heard the stories, but will say they are just that—stories. The story most associated with the hospital is the one in which second and third shift workers see a former nurse in the older part of the hospital checking on patients. This former RN was said to have died in the hospital.

I couldn't find one person who would admit having any firsthand knowledge of the nurse ghost, but one employee who has heard the stories said the nurse ghost was supposed to have worked in the *ER*.

Unexplained things have happened in numerous places in the hospital, not just the *ER*. Cabinet drawers fling open, blood pressure cuffs inflate automatically without anyone starting them, and call lights go off in unoccupied rooms—and these are just a few of the odd things that occur without the help of human hands.

One nurse, who worked at a different hospital before coming to Memorial, said she once saw a patient staring at her through a window (in her former hospital). This patient had cotton stuffed in his nostrils that was tied around his head. It was then that she realized the man was dead. The patient disappeared an instant later.

The same nurse heard a story that supposedly happened at Memorial before she got there. She heard that a teenage girl who had come to visit her sick mother, felt a hand on her shoulder when she was in the hallway. When she turned around, she saw her mother. Confused because her mother was supposed to be in bed, she took a step forward, into the room to see how her mother had escaped the tangle of equipment. Her mother was in bed, asleep. Later that day, the girl's mother died.

Memorial is located at 313 Stoughton Road in Edgerton.

Milton House

Milton House, Milton.

Some say they get the "willies" just looking at the building—this despite the gigantic, commercial-looking "Milton House" painted across the side of the building.

The Milton House was constructed by Underground Railroad conductor, Joseph Goodrich. This building, featuring a hexagonal three-story tower, was once a local inn as well as the Goodrich family residence.

Goodrich was born in Massachusetts. His family was active in the Seventh Day Baptist Church, which officially denounced slavery in several resolutions.

This stagecoach inn was built in 1844, and is thought to be the oldest poured concrete building in the United States. Living quarters

and guest rooms were in the upper floors of the hexagon and wing. The ground floor of the Milton House housed a lobby, dining room, and businesses. A third floor was added to the hexagon in 1867.

The Milton House also consists of part of an original log cabin, country store, buggy shed, smokehouse, and blacksmith shop. The log cabin, built in 1837, once housed a tunnel to the Milton House and was a hideout for the Underground Railroad.

Many Wisconsinites don't know much about how the issue of slavery was handled here. In the beginning years, masters brought their slaves with them to Wisconsin. Some of the slaves were freed when they arrived in Wisconsin; others were taken to the lead mining areas of southwest Wisconsin to work in the mines. Southeast Wisconsin had strong abolitionist leanings. When the Fugitive Slave Law of 1850 was passed, it incited the passions of many Wisconsinites. Delegations in both houses of the state voted against its passage, and the law was condemned in political conventions in Waterford.

The Underground Railroad is believed to be the reason the building and grounds are haunted. The ghosts that haunt the buildings and grounds are thought to be slaves who either passed through or died here. The Goodrich family is also believed to have a presence here, watching over things as they did in life.

The building is located at 18 South Janesville Street in beautiful downtown Milton. The Milton House National Historic Landmark is on the National Register of Historic Places, National Park Service Underground Railroad Network to Freedom, and is also part of the Wisconsin Heritage Sign Program.

Lincoln—Tallman House

Lincoln-Tallman House, Janesville.

T he Lincoln-Tallman House is the only private Wisconsin home still standing in which Lincoln stayed. If you're in the Janesville area, and even if you're not, a tour of the house is well worth your time. Even if you don't like history, you can't help but be impressed with the sheer size and elegance of the stone structure.

The "Tallman" in Lincoln-Tallman House was a man very concerned with the political issues of his time. He detested slavery and was crusader for its abolition for thirty years. He found agreement

Impressive architecture.

View of the Lincoln-Tallman from across the Rock River.

in his view on temperance and the abolition of slavery with the expanding Republican Party. When he joined the Republican party, Abraham Lincoln was very active in the party in nearby Illinois.

While conducting a speaking tour in Wisconsin in 1859, Lincoln accepted an invitation to address the Janesville Republican Club. He spent the weekend of October 1-2 with the Tallmans in their new home, a twenty-six-room Italianate villa style mansion.

The house, made of Milwaukee cream brick, was an impressive 10,000 square feet in size, had an extensive running water system, and gasoliers that would light entire rooms before electricity was invented. In 1871, it was called the "finest and most costly residence in Wisconsin."

Some say they feel spirits in the house. It could be the spirits of the Tallman family, still helping runaway slaves, the slaves themselves, or even Abraham Lincoln. You can see this incredible house from across the Rock River. Perhaps the ghosts in the house check out the view from one of the top windows in the house.

The house is located at 440 North Jackson Street in Janesville. To find this incredible treasure, take exit 175A off I-90 (Highway 11), turn right on Franklin Street, turn left on Mineral Point Avenue, and turn left on Jackson. You will see the house and outbuildings on the left. The house still contains the bed Lincoln slept in.

Hotel Boscobel

This hotel was the very first meeting place of the Gideons International Society, and is touted as "Birthplace of the Gideon Bible!" (You know the ones I'm talking about—the little ones you find in the nightstand drawer of many hotels in the U.S.)

Adam Bobel, the hotel's builder, has been spotted in the hotel by staff and visitors, apparently still checking on his business affairs.

Bobel was born in Prussia in 1834. He emigrated to the United States in 1853, married in 1855, and made Boscobel his home in 1861. When the Civil War broke out, he became a sutler; a vendor approved by the government and licensed to a regiment or post.

In 1865, Bobel and a man named Mr. Schaffer, built a two-story stone building in Boscobel for use as a saloon. This is now the southern portion of the hotel.

Bobel purchased Schaffer's interest in the saloon and began running it alone. In 1873, Bobel built onto the saloon. It was a big three-story structure that extended over the original saloon building.

A fire gutted the building in 1881. Only the walls and the sign remained standing. Bobel rebuilt the hotel in only four months' time. It was now known as the Central House.

This is when and where the Gideons International Society story gets its start. Because there were no rooms available in the then Central House, traveling salesman, John H. Nicholson, was asked to share a room with another salesman, Samuel E. Hill. The two men discussed the need for an organization that could provide "mutual help and recognition for Christian travelers." The two men met again a year later and were joined by another salesman. The result: The organization known as the Christian Commercial Travelers' Association of America was founded.

Adam Bobel operated the hotel until his death. Incredibly, the exterior of the hotel today looks pretty much like it did in 1881.

Bobel died in 1885, but he's still a familiar sight to guests and employees more than a hundred years later.

Elsing's Second Hand Shop

Elsing's Second Hand Shop, Stoughton. *Courtesy of Phillip and Vicky Elsing.*

This incredible second hand shop, located on 421 East Main Street in Stoughton, was built in 1891. In the beginning, it was the Hanson House/Grand Hotel, which also served as a brothel and saloon. At one point in its history, it was also a grocery store, teen center, and pizza place.

The Elsing specialize in the sale of used furniture, household goods, toys, books, and collectibles—they put the big building to good use. The first floor is used for merchandise display, utilities, and storage. The third floor, which once housed twenty-seven hotel rooms, is a large open space, used for storage.

Like a number of other former hotels, brothels, and saloons, Elsing's Second Hand Shop, has ghosts. What makes Elsing's Second Hand Shop so unique is the amount of documented paranormal activity. Vicky and her husband, Philip, have had many mediums and paranormal groups investigate the ghosts in their building. The Elsings hope they will someday learn why the ghosts are there and what is needed for them to move on.

Vicky Elsing isn't afraid to work in the store, though she admits she's not too keen on the idea of going there at night, alone. Like many others who share part of their life with a ghost or ghosts, she loves owning a haunted business, yet still has days where the ghosts cause her a little anxiety.

"I have gotten very used to the spirits in my shop," she writes in her blog. "Nothing bad has ever happened to me or anyone that I know. So tell me why do I always have this strange feeling to look behind me. Why am I so afraid of what is behind me? Why am I so afraid that

Building in 1891. *Courtesy of Philip and Vicky Elsing.*

someone is going to reach out and touch me with my back turned? I always get this feeling when I'm down stairs at night shutting up the shop and turning off the lights, getting ready to go home. Why am I so afraid of the dark when I'm alone? I'm not afraid of the dark in my house; I'm not even afraid of being home alone at night in my home. So why does my building make me feel this way?"

This is a sentiment many feel when they are alone in a place believed to be haunted. Vicky doesn't belong to any paranormal groups; she didn't even know what the word "paranormal" meant until things—odd things—started happening at the shop. It was then that she did some research and began contacting those associated with paranormal investigations.

In the 1970s, when the building was a teen center, Vicky's friend, Pam Buckley, saw an image of a girl or woman who wore a long white dress and had curly hair. The girl just might be the same ghost a medium saw there recently. The medium says the girl's name is Mary. Mary was the daughter of a hotel worker. In an audio file, the medium asks if anyone else is in the room. Moments later, what is believed to be "Just me," can be heard.

During one investigation, a rocking chair started rocking in the furniture room. The team asked the little girl ghost (Mary) if she was with them and could she turn the pages of the book. (Mary likes to be read to.) The pages started moving. At first everyone thought one of the investigators might be causing it. When the investigator put her face inside her shirt to breathe, the book pages still lifted up—at one point, almost straight up and down. During this investigation, the temperature underwent some noticeable changes, too: from 71 up to 81, and then back down to about 68 degrees again. Incredibly, even when the temperature was 81 degrees, everyone in the room was cold.

Paranormal groups and mediums have provided the Elsings with evidence and information about the ghosts in the building, including EVPs. In one audio file, two mediums claim the voices of two ghosts can be heard. One is of a man; the other of a girl, crying. Could this be Mary again?

A short rundown of some of the not-quite-so-ordinary happenings at Elsing's: muffled voices and the sound of a child crying in the basement, whispering heard in your ear in various places in the building, a ceramic figurine splitting in half on its own, black swirling shadows

in the basement, items being found in the middle of an aisle in the morning, when the building was checked before being locked for the night, items floating off upstairs in the "kitchen" area, the "book room" door in the basement opening on its own and unlocking numerous times (now locked to prevent this from happening again), a two-way radio crackling and then blowing up while in someone's hand, numerous cold spots throughout the building, Otis (their dog) growling and barking at nothing, the sound of crying, and orbs captured on film and seen in person. Talk about a list!

There are other ghosts besides Mary that are believed to haunt the shop: Margaret, believed to have been a prostitute, and two men named Simon and Henry.

In the 1920s, when the building was a brothel, it was known as the kingpin of bootlegging in Stoughton. One story concerning the building focuses on a former sheriff and chief of police, Saxe Hoverson, who fell from a third-story window. When he fell, some speculated that it was a suicide attempt. He died a few days later, but his injuries, which included a skull fracture, broken ribs and ankles, caused others to believe he may have been "helped" out the window. This might not be such a far-fetched idea. Wisconsin served as an outlet and haven for Chicago-area gangsters such as "Terrible" Touhey and Al Capone during the bootlegging days of Prohibition.

Philip and Vicky Elsing. *Courtesy of Philip and Vicky Elsing.*

Otis. *Courtesy of Philip and Vicky Elsing.*

Audio and sightings aren't the extent of the reported haunting. Vicky has a black and white photograph she believes shows a ghostly head, hair, eyes, shoulders, and arms.

Do the ghosts at Elsing's like all the attention they've been getting? Maybe not so much. During one investigation, Mary (the girl ghost) told a psychic that she and some of the other spirits felt the building was starting to feel like a circus, with people coming in at all hours. The little girl ghost said they (the spirits) were getting "tired of performing for the groups." Vicky, a caring soul, promptly stopped all "ghost hunts" for a while to give her ghostly inhabitants a break.

Want to learn what's new in the paranormal world as it applies to the secondhand shop? Elsing keeps all findings posted near the cash register. The building, located south of Lake Kegonsa along the Yahara River (which, through larger tributaries feeds into the Gulf of Mexico), is only twenty-five minutes southeast of Madison. Its location near the Yahara River is something that has been noted by paranormal investigators; some experts believe that energy forms can use moving water as a type of conduit.

Haunted rocking chair. *Courtesy of Philip and Vicky Elsing.*

Beaver Dam Area Community Theatre

This ghost story is unusual because it not only reveals the identity of the ghost, it tells how the ghost came to be a ghost.

It would have been nice to know the state of mind of the girl in this story, but this is something that I haven't been able to find out. I also haven't been able to verify that this event even took place, but it's a story that is well known in Beaver Dam, and also believed—the basis of any good ghost story. All stories, ghost or not, have at least a kernel of truth.

The Beaver Dam Area Community Theatre building was formerly the First Baptist Church. Acquired in 1983, it is said to provide an ideal intimate theater with excellent acoustics. The building has two floors of work, storage, and performance space.

The ghost of this story most likely spent part of her last earthly day thinking about acting. Tryouts for a play were taking place that fateful night. She, a young girl, came to the theater, tried out, and didn't make it.

Distraught, and dare I say angry, she was said to have gone up to the loft of the theater. Once there, she made a noose and proceeded to hang herself. It seems a rather strong and rather odd way to deal with rejection, but as I mentioned before, who knows what state of mind the girl was in before she came to try out for the play?

The girl ghost's name is said to be Lacy. Reports of a light going out in the loft, as well as the sound of footsteps running up the stairs accompanied by crying, are the foundation of this story.

The building's main stage and balcony levels contain 219 "comfortable theater seats." The theater's Web site says nothing about a ghost. It does, however, mention a lot of really great past and upcoming productions—none containing the word "ghost."

The Beaver Dam Area Community Theatre is located at 219 North Spring Street in Beaver Dam.

Quickie

Ghost Stories!

Bartell Community Theatre

Bartell Theatre, Madison.

T his retro-looking building stands at 113 East Mifflin Street, just a few blocks from the Capitol. While it's the type of building that probably wouldn't make you stop and take a second look if you didn't know what it was, the story about its haunted interior just might.

Before it was the Bartell Community Theatre, it was the former Esquire Theatre. The then-creative director of the Strollers Theatre was alone in the building, working on the renovation of the balcony. As he worked, he heard someone in the auditorium below him whistling the theme song to Paint Your Wagon.

The creative director called out that the theme song was one of his favorites. After hearing no response from the auditorium, he realized no one was there. At least no one that was alive.

The creative director, who didn't believe in ghosts, was nonetheless frightened by the experience. The first manager of the theater was said to have died in the building. Many that have visited the theater say they've felt a cold breeze blow by when there is no reason for it. Some have reported hearing footsteps when no one is around. Could it be the manager checking things out?

Interestingly, the first movie played at the Esquire—Paint Your Wagon.

Dyreson Road

I n the mood for a little driving drama? Perhaps a little (literal) spin on the bridge? You just might encounter both if you drive down haunted Dyreson Road.

Screams and cries coming from the bridge are a regular occurrence, and if you're lucky, you might just see cars hanging from the bridge. Huh?! According to more than one teenager, cars have been seen "dangling over the side of the bridge" before they disappeared.

The crying, screaming, and car danglings aren't the only odd stories associated with Dyreson Road. Eye witnesses have seen an old black car appear behind their car. This black car is then said to quickly close the gap. As you watch it get closer and closer, you're sure it's going to ram you. When you close your eyes and brace for impact, the car is gone.

When I asked teens in the area about this story, they all said it was true. Not one of them had witnessed any strange sights. Two girls said they had heard thin screams, but they weren't sure if they were ghostly or not.

Bourbon Street Grille

Bourbon Street Grille, Monona.

This haunted restaurant, located on the Yahara River, at 6312 Metropolitan Lane in Monona, was formerly known as Muskie Lounge, Crab House, and Four Lakes Yacht Club.

It is believed to have only one ghost in residence—a former employee who's been dead for years. When she was alive, she was a waitress at the Four Lakes Yacht Club. Her name was Marlene and she had a heart attack during her Friday night shift. She died later, but apparently loved her job so much that she continues to come to work every day. That's dedication.

Employees feel someone tapping on their shoulders and feminine laughter when there's no one there.

In fact, Marlene is so dedicated to her work that she has taken it upon herself to let her opinion be known—at least as far as her work environment goes. When the restaurant underwent remodeling, nothing went according to plan. Things would be laid out and the next day, things would be a mess. Equipment failed for no reason.

The ghostly waitress has also tossed pots and pans to the floor and is believed to be responsible for helping visiting bands unpack their equipment.

Apparently Marlene has a soft spot for musicians.

Waubesa Street Ghost

I have to admit I was skeptical when I read accounts of a haunting at the tracks on Waubesa Street near the Lowell Elementary School located at 401 Maple Avenue. It sounds like the kind of story kids tell to scare other kids.

In one version of the story, a little girl ghost haunts the area between Waubesa Street and Division Street. Nearby residents tell stories of ghostly encounters and say the little girl is responsible. No one knows who the little girl was, or if she was killed on the tracks or a different tragedy, or if she died of natural causes or an illness.

Another story about the little girl is that she moves through homes in the neighborhood eating snacks and leaving the remnants as proof she was there.

The other story that involves a ghost child near the Waubesa tracks features a little boy. This boy was supposedly killed by a train. You don't see the boy unless you park your car on the tracks at midnight. First you hear blood dripping on your car (apparently ghosts can bleed) and then you see the boy ghost hovering over your car.

I'm told there are two sets of tracks that could be haunted. No one is quite sure which set of tracks the little boy haunts. One set of tracks is said to be north of Kupfer's Iron Works (now the Kupfer Center), the other just south. The north set of tracks are on an abrupt rise in the road that borders the south side of Wirth Court Park. The second set of tracks seems most likely because they are on a nearly flat portion of the road, which is easy for a child to walk and ride a bicycle over.

Adults remember when they were children and having the crossing guard stationed east of Waubesa Street give stern warnings about leaving their shoe behind if their foot got caught and there was a train coming. It was probably just a motherly warning, but maybe the guard was remembering a previous accident. The little boy or girl ghost, perhaps?

Mickey's Tavern

This bar, located just off the west bank of the Yahara River at 1524 Williamson Street, is believed to be haunted. The place itself has been described by pub crawlers as unique. People drive from as far away as Milwaukee to join in and play at the improv Celtic music jam sessions. The tavern's past, however, is not all music and joy.

Someone, who was said to have been murdered years ago on the front steps of Mickey's, is said to haunt the bar today. Others believe the owner is the one who haunts the bar.

The former owner, who died a few years ago, was said to live in the same building. Even though he was in his 90s and barely able to walk, he would come downstairs and watch over his bar.

After he died, renovations began and drastic changes were made. The apartment that the owner used to live in was opened up and is now part of the bar area. A sitting room and pool table room are now part of the décor.

It is not known if the former owner approves or disapproves of the changes; only that when the place is calm, you get the feeling that another presence is nearby.

Mendota Mental Health Institute and Governor's Island

Mendota Mental Health Institute on Troy Drive and nearby Governor's Island are located in naturally beautiful places. They're also haunted if you believe the stories of those who have seen otherworldly animals that prowl the area. A ghostly black panther has been spotted near Troy Drive on the northern shore of Lake Mendota.

Farwell's Point Mound Group and Mendota State Historical Mound Group are prominent features of this area. Like many other sites that have been built over or around Native American burial mounds, the cries of ghostly eagles can sometimes be heard.

Some have seen or have had strong visions of Native Americans in traditional dress that disappear after a few moments.

Others in this area have seen misty figures that are larger than the size of a human. Most report feeling the sensation they are not alone. Some say they get the feeling that someone doesn't want them there.

Stoughton Hospital

This modern-looking hospital has a couple ghostly stories associated with it. Employees there say they have seen the ghost of a patient who died there. The patient is said to be in his early 20s and is always dressed in a hospital gown.

Employees say this former patient causes call lights to go on in empty rooms, and speaks to nurses as a human (not a ghost) that is not registered at the hospital.

The second story involves an upper floor in the hospital. One source says it's the second floor, another says it's the third floor. A ghostly presence is said to move past you in one certain room. It is not known whether the presence was a former patient, a visitor, or even a former hospital worker. The presence is not threatening.

The final story involves a woman who came to visit her daughter and newborn grandson at the hospital. She says she rode in the elevator with a friendly woman and they even chitchatted about weather. When it was time for the elevator doors to open, the woman had disappeared into thin air.

The experience shook up the woman so much she had to sit down. She never told her daughter about the encounter; her daughter doesn't believe in ghosts—except in the movies.

Muscoda's Ghosts

Muscoda is billed as "Morel Mushroom Capital of Wisconsin." Its ghosts usually get second-billing. At least for now.

Muscoda is a little village northwest of Madison. People talk about a murder that supposedly occurred in this former mining town years ago. One resident said the murder was likely the result of a number of things: Decades ago the mining veins began to dry up. It was at that time that cholera was also responsible for many deaths in the area. And last but not least, fortunes were likely won and lost, causing some drastic actions.

Those who have driven through the town say "there's something just not right" about it. Despite a normal appearance, you get the chills and the feeling you are being watched the whole time you are there.

Another explanation for this feeling might be due to the fact that there are many effigy mounds in the area. The area may have had a special significance to the Native Americans who lived there long ago.

Some unusual ghosts have been seen and reported in Muscoda. One is the ghost of a man wearing an old-time sheriff's outfit at the dam. He is said to look out at the water at night. He might sound like a tranquil sort, but he's been spotted many times where teenagers hold parties. Apparently, he doesn't like the tranquility of the area disturbed. Partiers beware.

The second sighting deals with a transparent woman in the Blue River Sand Barrens State Natural Area. She is said to hover near a boulder. Some of the residents of Muscoda say it is the spirit of a woman who was murdered while driving through Muscoda long ago.

Another ghost that has been mentioned is dressed as a "cowboy" who rides on the outskirts of town. No mention of the horse he was riding, or if he carried a gun.

And finally, this area, like Blue Mounds, has had many sightings of the watcher. Most of these sightings include men in military dress.

Bay View Townhouses

Haunted. Not haunted.

Some that live here say the rumors of ghosts of Bay View Townhouses are just that—rumors. Others say they not only believe ghosts exist here, they've seen the mists and shadows that prove it. Not only that, they've taken pictures in the parking lot that have ended up with smears or white orbs.

While it hasn't been substantiated, some say the townhouses sit on top of a Native American burial ground. This isn't surprising; many burial grounds are in the Madison area.

Some say they've seen a little girl dressed in white at the basketball court here, crying for her mother.

La Follette High School

This high school is regarded as haunted because of one thing and one thing only: the auditorium.

For years, those in the auditorium and the classrooms directly behind the auditorium, told of being alone, but not being alone.

Students report having the hair on their neck and arms raise in this area. They also report getting the feeling that someone or something is looking at them, even though there's no one in sight.

If you're like me, that would be all it would take to hightail it outta there.

If you do hang around, this is the point where you just might hear footsteps. These usually always belong to someone with an invisible everything.

One of last things you might witness if you happen to find yourself still rooted to the spot, is the auditorium curtains opening or closing on their own.

If you visit the school's Web site and click on a map of the school, you might—or might not—be surprised to see a "Cemetery" located directly behind the school. Could this be the reason for the ghostly curtain manipulator?

Maple Bluff Country Club

L ocation. Location. Location. The address 500 Kensington Drive just might be the underlying reason this place is reported to have ghosts.

Maple Bluff, population 1,380, is located on a narrow band of land on the northeast shoreline of Lake Mendota where the Winnebago Indians once had their summer encampments. Hmmm. A former Native American encampment—usually a good indication a little spiritual interaction might be headed your way.

Apparently, it doesn't matter if you're paying over $4,000 per year in membership fees. If a ghost wants to haunt a place, it's going to haunt it.

Getting a real live person to admit to seeing a ghost here is akin to pulling teeth. Past staff members have admitted to seeing ghosts on the well-manicured grounds. Clients have admitted to seeing ghosts at the club. Does that mean there are ghosts at this upscale country club?

I'm thinking so.

McNeel Middle School

A written account of the haunting of this school seems to have been prepared by a student that either attends or has attended the school. I haven't been able to get any more information beyond posts on the Internet, but I'm including this because it is a site of interest to amateur ghost hunters and paranormal researchers.

McNeel Middle School is located at 1524 Frederick Street on Beloit's northwest side. The outside of the school doesn't give a clue that it's haunted, but, like many other sites, looks don't mean much when it comes to hauntings and ghosts.

The story about McNeel haunting is unlike other school haunting stories in that a lot of bad things are said to happen or have happened there.

The first part of the story deals with the backroom of the stage. Costumes are stored there and students sometimes gather there to do homework or talk. This spot in the school is supposedly where the man that haunts the school used to live.

Buckle up. This is where the story takes a dark, sharp turn. The theater teacher was sleeping on the couch and when she awoke, there was blood everywhere. Turns out an electricity plug was plugged into the back of her head.

The same "ghost" responsible for the theater teacher's woes is also believed to be the same entity that writes on the wall mirror and slams the door. But wait, there's more. There's also a chalkboard in the room. The number "666" will be "scratched into it" and there's no way to erase it. Then, a few days later it will disappear only to reappear later.

The room is very quiet, and a dark feeling comes over you when you're in there. Probably a subtle warning—ceiling tiles fall down in this room. According to the report this happens often. Luckily, the tiles fall down moments after the person that had been standing below them moves away.

Flynn's Steakhouse

T he old building that houses the steakhouse is said to be one of the oldest buildings in Brodhead. It is a restaurant now, but once was a hotel. It was during the time that it was a hotel that it got its haunting reputation.

Many residents of Brodhead believe the restaurant is haunted because they have seen objects moving by themselves and heard noises that defy explanation.

Flynn's Steakhouse is located at 1101 1st Center Avenue in Brodhead.

Dodgeville Subway

Subway, Dodgeville.

I t looks like an ordinary Subway sandwich shop inside and out. But it's what you can't see that makes this Subway so much different than any other Subway. Ghosts.

The logical question to ask would be who or what haunts this relatively new restaurant. The logical answer just might be its location. Dodgeville and nearby Mineral Point are ghost-rich.

Dodgeville ghosts associated with the corner of Clarence and Union Streets have been around the area a long time—since 1828. That's when pioneers began being buried—on the site of a Native American burial ground.

The spirits that haunt the graveyard have shown their presence in a number of ways. Some aren't so nice. Reports of screaming-face apparitions and withered corpses are just a few of the ways these ghosts say hello. These same horrifying sights have been seen on and around Highway 23, where Subway is located.

The ghost or ghosts that haunt Subway may not get in your face, but they still enjoy the same kind of mischief the graveyard ghosts enjoy. It's said if you go downstairs after nine o'clock at night, all kinds of strange things start to happen.

Things will leap off shelves and fall to the floor. But wait, it gets worse. An extreme stench will fill the building. It's so bad you can't stand it; it's worse than death.

The ghosts are said to enjoy setting off the door beepers—a lot. Employees have heard their name being called out by an invisible someone or something.

A couple of employees have seen a skinny woman wearing a dress, about fifty years old standing by the register. She was wearing a frown. Hungry perhaps? When an employee went to the register, she vanished.

Milton High School

The ghosts of two old teachers who died when the school caught fire in the 1960s are said to haunt this high school. They've only been seen in these rooms: 145-148.

If you sit at a desk in one of the aforementioned rooms, a ghosts is said to walk past and give you an "evil" look, which will of course make you feel odd. I mean, how couldn't it?

If you can tear your glance away and take a gander at the blackboard, you might see the names of children written on it. These are the children the two teachers punished. If you try to erase them, you can't.

Try not to make any sudden moves. If you scream or jump up, the teachers will disappear.

Another spot in the high school that is said to be haunted is the auditorium which was just built. If you are seated, you can sometimes hear the curtains open partially and then fall to the floor on their own.

Can You Keep A Secret?

"I don't believe in ghosts. There is no such thing."

This blunt statement comes from a man who only believes what he can see or prove, despite the fact that family members have had spiritual and paranormal experiences they totally believe. His wife calls herself spiritual with a healthy dose of practicality built in. The kicker: He's had experiences he can't explain with conventional methods—yet he still stubbornly believes things like ghosts and psychic experiences, etc. are a product of your imagination.

That's why a recent experience he had is so remarkable. It disturbed him so much, he shared the story, even though he felt a little foolish and said he never wanted to talk about it again.

"It was 8:30 in the morning. I was wide awake in bed and thinking about getting up. I was lying on my side facing the wall. I didn't hear my wife breathing like she does when she's asleep, so I wasn't sure if she was sleeping or awake like I was.

"Suddenly I felt the mattress move just behind me. I felt soft breathing on my neck and then heard: 'Can you keep a secret?'"

He remembers wondering why his wife would say such a thing, and why she had picked such an odd time to tell him. The soft breathing at his neck continued.

He admits the question disturbed him, but not as much as the soft breathing on his neck. Suddenly irritated, he turned around to ask his wife what she was talking about.

His wife was facing the other way, at least 2-3 feet away from him! His first thought was: *What the hell?!*

He jumped out of bed, struggling to figure out what just happened. He knows he was wide awake and not dreaming. He knows what he heard, and he knows the breath he felt on his neck was warm and real.

Does this mean he now believes there are things out there that may defy logical or scientific explanation?

The question is met with a resolute, "No!"

Lake View Cemetery at Warner Park

Warner Park is located at 1625 Northport Drive on Madison's northeast side. The park is said to sit on Native American burial grounds. Some people experience odd "feelings" when they are in certain spots in the park itself, but it's the cemetery that is considered haunted.

Lake View Graveyard was established in 1858. At that time it was most likely surrounded by marsh and farmland. Visit the cemetery during the day and you may, or may not, get the feeling the graveyard is haunted.

Visit the graveyard at night and you will most likely get the feeling it is haunted. Even if you only get strange vibes while you're there, the photos you check out later will most likely contain things you may have only dreamed of capturing.

Many anomalies in various colors have been reported in photographs taken at night. These shapes and streaks were not tiny; some literally filled the photograph.

The identity of the graveyard haunter is a mystery.

The Narrows

The Narrows, Sauk County.

I f you drive west into Baraboo, you might pass by the historical marker without giving it a second look—or thought. But this spot on the side of a curve in the road, across from a bluff, is said to be inhabited by many spirits.

Just behind the marker is a marshy area. Huge farms encircle this spot that is said to be filled with the spirits of Native Americans who once called it home.

The bluff across the road is the rumored home of animals no longer living. Some say they've heard the so-close-it's-scary screech of an eagle, yet no eagle nests are visible from The Narrows.

Others have described wind that comes off the bluff, flattens the grass, and blows toward The Narrows where it disappears into the

trees. If you are in its path, you will not be harmed, but you will feel the hair on the back of your neck rise. No one really knows what this strong, dense, cold wind represents, but it's an anomaly. Often there is no wind elsewhere in the area.

Some people link The Narrows to the narrows in Wisconsin Dells, not too far north of this spot. The Dells' narrows are said to be one of the most haunted spots in Wisconsin.

Even in winter, with the sun shining, you get a strange feeling here. Swirls of cold air circle up and around some visitors. Some feel someone standing right behind them, but when they turn around, no one is there.

University of Wisconsin
and On Wisconsin!

UW—Whitewater

U W—Whitewater is located at 800 West Main Street in Whitewater. One thing I learned while researching the campus, is the town of Whitewater is thought to be "creepy" and "downright dangerous." It's even referred to as "Second Salem," but since this book is about ghosts, I'll leave well enough alone—unless I hear that the witches there can also turn into ghosts.

Some of the ghosts of the Whitewater campus are attributed to specific entities, as I'll describe in a moment. Other people believe the area is haunted because the land near Tripp and Cravath Lakes was responsible for the destruction of many sacred Native American burial mounds.

Truth be told, Whitewater has a strange past. Poisonings, UFO sightings, ice floes on area lakes in the summertime, evidence of satanic rituals, and tentacled lake creatures are just some of the things you read about when you research this picturesque town—ghosts just might be the least worrisome thing you might encounter.

I'm giving you fair warning, just in case.

Calvary Cemetery

Calvary Cemetery is located on a hill above the campus. Freshmen are warned to stay away; the gates close on those that venture inside at night. At least that's the story.

An axe murderess named Mary Worth is said to be buried there. It's reported that she leaves her grave every Halloween and roams the dormitory halls wielding her axe.

Cabin on the Hill

School officials deny reports the cabin is haunted, yet stories continue to circulate about a young ghost who can be seen looking out the window. Many current students say the stories are true. No one has been harmed by this window-peeker-outer. Yet.

Library

The UW-Whitewater library contains some really intense books. Included in their collection is a book on the sublevel that has the power to make you commit suicide if you read it. The death tally so far: three students. A janitor got off lucky. He wound up at the asylum. No names have been assigned to the victims, but every year around Halloween, the library staff gets the same questions regarding these "killer" books and supposed victims. *Army of Darkness* anyone?

Green Hill Center of the Arts

After hours students have heard hammering in the metals lab when no one is present within. Students have seen chairs moving across the room by themselves, and shadows that flit along the walls.

Clem Hall

People can be heard running in the halls when the halls are empty; bathroom stall doors slam at night; there's talking and laughing in the halls when no one is there; and during homecoming week, a ghostly figure has been inside Clem that disappears if you stare at it long enough.

Fricker Hall

On certain nights, and no one was specific what nights these were, a ghost of a student can be seen walking in the basement. I've heard it is a young woman, and I've been told it is young man. Either way, a ghost is a ghost; frightening to behold to some, a dream come true to others.

Knilans Hall

This hall is haunted by a librarian who died there. The librarian apparently was a very helpful person. One student reported two regular doors and an elevator door opening for her when she had her arms full of books.

Sorority House and Other Dormitories

One sorority house was the former home of one of the deans. His daughter hung herself there. It's believed the room the girl

hung herself in is haunted. Those who stay in the room feel a strong sense of unease; some are so frightened they move out.

Another sorority house located at 614 West Main sits on top of a tunnel that reportedly served the Underground Railroad. The young women of the Alpha Sigma sorority were distracted from dinner one night in 1981 by noises coming from the basement. Until that night, they didn't know a tunnel existed. They found the floor covered with debris and bricks that had somehow broken free of the boarded-up tunnel entrance. Or perhaps it was an exit for something unearthly…

Another dorm, no name could be found, reportedly has people buried right-side up beneath it.

Witnesses living in the Delta Zeta House have heard someone or something walking down the large front staircase, making creaking sounds as it progresses.

I'll finish strong with Wells Hall dormitory, built in the late 1960s. This is the most talked about place on campus. Supposedly a sacrificial altar, along with the several dead coven members are said to be buried behind Wells Hall.

Oddly enough, the hauntings reported in or near Wells are usually said to be young adults who died in heartbreaking accidents, rather than coven ghosts. Maybe coven members are too busy in the afterlife casting spells to haunt a dorm that didn't mean anything to them in life.

UW—Madison

UW—Whitewater campus is creepy, but of all the campuses in Wisconsin, Madison is without a doubt, the most haunted. Nearly every building on campus and those associated with the school that aren't on the immediate grounds have multiple stories of ghostly encounters and hauntings.

The UW campus, including the Arboretum, is home to twenty-two archeological sites. Many of these include Ho-Chunk burial mounds. Eagle Heights woods, Picnic Point, and Observatory Hill are spots where members of the Mississippian culture lived more than a thousand years ago.

There are so many encounters and sightings, in fact, that the Wisconsin Alumni Association compiled a number of those stories. These stories are similar to those still told today, yet much, much more detailed and frightening.

The following are general stories about the ghosts on and around the Madison campus. Stories from alumni featured in *On Wisconsin* magazine appear later in the book. Enjoy them all!

Tunnel Bob

Tunnel Bob is/was a real person. If you're wondering why I used present and past tense, it's because I haven't been able to get a definitive answer on whether Tunnel Bob is still alive or if he died long ago.

He was a regular sight in downtown Madison. He used to go into cafés and order coffee—but that was a few decades ago. He was most famous for traversing the steam tunnels beneath the campus. P.S. This is a big no-no! Don't even think about it! You will get a *biiiiiig* fine.

Here's what is known about the Tunnel Bob of UW—Madison (there's a Tunnel Bob of Madison East High School, too, by the way).

There are two sets of tunnels that comprise the UW's heating system: from the Memorial library to Weisman Center, and Lake Mendota to University Avenue. The maze of steam tunnels has been

active since the late 1800s. The idea of steam tunnels sounds archaic, but there are still universities in the United States and Europe that use steam.

Tunnel Bob patrolled the steam tunnels for at least forty years. The tunnels are off-limits to the general public, and one more time: Trespassers will be given a **stiff fine**. Besides the monetary lose, there are other things you might want to consider. There's the danger of asbestos in the tunnels as well as the danger of a pipe bursting. I don't know anyone who can outrun scalding 430° steam spraying from a pipe. Or a ghost.

Those that have gone into the tunnels haven't stayed long. There's usually dirty blankets, heat, and a general feeling of claustrophobic filth. Those that enter the tunnel with flashlights get freaked out that others in the dark tunnels can see them, but they can't see who's just past their light. There's also that inescapable feeling that someone is breathing down your neck, willing you to go away.

Tunnel Bob, when he was alive (and he still might be) was described by some as homeless, and others as having a home. He had money to purchase mochas from the coffee shops around campus, and was believed to be autistic, so it would follow that he had a home and a caregiver. While not the most social being, Tunnel Bob never hurt anyone, though he was said to have been kicked out of the tunnels for several months because of threatening behavior.

One thing that is a certainty: Tunnel Bob had burns from the steam pipes of the university's steam pipes. He was conscientious, too; he left notes for UW maintenance workers indicating what needed to be repaired or replaced in the tunnels.

He was said to be tall and thin and in the habit of wearing a blue coat. When he was seen on the streets of Madison, he was said to walk with one foot on the sidewalk and the other on the grass.

Students, when polled about Tunnel Bob, are divided. The majority say he's dead and is said to haunt the tunnels below campus. There are a few that insist Tunnel Bob is still alive.

Despite no real answer, the tunnels below UWM are said to be haunted. If Tunnel Bob is not the spirit patrolling the tunnels, it could a number of other possibilities: the spirit of a homeless person who perhaps perished here, or a Native American spirit...or even a student who foolishly decided to check out the tunnels.

Helen C. White Hall

Despite the fact that Helen C. White died in 1967 and the hall wasn't built until two years later overlooking Lake Mendota, the hall is reputedly haunted by the L&S professor, a true Wisconsin trailblazer.

Today the hall houses the English Department, College Library, and other L&S department offices.

When White was alive, she was beloved by students, who called her the "Purple Goddess" because of the color of her wardrobe. She is fondly remembered by former students.

Some say they get a whiff of lilac when no one else is around. The color of purple lilacs, as well as the scent, are said to have been White's favorites.

Bascom Hall

The Lincoln statue at Bascom Hall has long been considered haunted. Two men—of the ghostly persuasion—have been seen standing alongside or behind Lincoln.

These ghostly men, sometimes both young, and sometimes one young and one old, are startling to behold, but don't seem menacing. The two are believed to be William Nelson, who died of typhoid in 1837, and Samuel Warren, who was struck by lightning in 1838 while working on construction of the Capitol.

Two metal squares to the left of the Abraham Lincoln statue mark their final resting places. Students walk across the graves every day, most without knowing what lies beneath their feet.

"Old Man Bascom" himself is said to haunt the hall which bears his name. "Sometimes I get the feeling someone's looking over my shoulder and then I feel an icy breeze. Everyone says it's Old Man Bascom telling me he's not very happy with me," one student told me when asked about her experience at Bascom Hall.

Music Hall

The Union Theatre, in particular, is believed to be haunted because many people have felt someone brush up against them, when there wasn't anyone around.

Students have also reported that electronic equipment turns on and off and on without the help of human hands. Others have reported hearing "scuffling" in the balcony when it was deserted.

North Hall

Sightings of ghosts are regularly reported by security and students alike. Doors—heavy doors—open at will. Once the door is open, a cold draft will assault whoever is on the other side.

North Hall opened in 1851; it was the first building erected on campus. It truly was an all-in-one building. It contained a library, living quarters, laboratories, chapel, and lecture rooms.

A student who saw the ghost at North Hall said he's never been so frightened in all his life. Though he knows others who have seen the ghost, he asked to remain anonymous so he doesn't "sound like a freak."

"I was walking up the stairwell when I looked up. At first I thought it was a well-dressed janitor, deep in thought or something. I guess I realized he wasn't human after a few seconds. I couldn't exactly look through him, but he wasn't solid," he recalls. "I wanted to run back down the stairs, but my legs wouldn't work, and this guy just kept coming. He wasn't looking at me, but was headed straight for me. So I did the only thing I could think of: I held my breath. He walked past or through me—I'm not sure which. When he passed by me, I felt like someone threw a bucket of snow on me. When I turned around, he was gone."

North Hall is filled with ghost sightings, usually that of a well-dressed man standing next to a custodian, or walking down the hall solo.

The man is believed to be a Political Science professor who had died of a heart attack while working late one night in the 1950s or 1960s.

Picnic Point

Visitors to the area have had experiences that include visions and very graphic psychic images of violence.

Radio Hall

Students, present and former, report having seen a ghost darting through the basement, especially in the hallways.

Other reports of the basement of Radio Hall being haunted involve a walk-in cooler that once held cadavers from Science Hall. Students have sworn they've seen ghosts walking through the basement. Looking for their earthly body, perhaps?

All throughout Radio Hall, the feeling that someone is watching you is a feeling that persists today. Many that walk through Radio Hall, especially the lower level, report cold breezes that defy logical explanation.

Sterling Hall

A professor (some say it was an assistant) was killed in one of the science labs as a statement against the Vietnam War. The spirit of the man killed is said to haunt the hall.

The feelings some get when they stop for a moment are of sadness and disappointment. Whether this is caused by the presence of the ghost of the man killed there, or individual thoughts about the senseless killing, the feeling is very real.

There's another ghost said to haunt Sterling Hall. The ghost of beautiful Christine Rothschild, a student at UW, who was murdered on campus in the late 1960s, is said to haunt this building. She lived at Ann Emery Hall, but her spirit is said to be felt most strongly here.

Memorial Library

Many students have locked themselves in the cages in the stacks. Why? To get some work done! One student remembers a number of different times working in different cages when the single light bulb would go out, and always at the worst possible moment, usually a really intense moment. He said it happened way too often to be coincidence.

Memorial Union, UW-Madison campus.

Science Hall, UW-Madison campus.

One student who worked in the library said books would regularly appear on table tops and then disappear—when no one was in the area.

Memorial Union

The second floor of this building is said to be haunted. An old lady (sometimes said to be a young lady), dressed in 1800s clothing, has been seen standing at the top of the stairs that lead to the pool hall. Others have seen "light colored" shadows "float" down hallways. Two workers are rumored to have died when a wall collapsed during construction.

The ghost that haunts the Wisconsin Union Theatre, the beautiful hall in Memorial Union, has been seen by many. A single ghost in white is usually preceded by a loud backstage noise, almost as if to get your attention. Then it moves across the stage, pausing in the middle, and then disappears.

The ghost could be a number of people since a number of people have died in the theater, including performers. The Minneapolis

Symphony Orchestra played here in 1950, and a drummer suffered a heart attack onstage. This happened just before intermission. The drummer managed to crawl offstage, but died before a doctor from the audience could reach him. Oddly, the rest of the orchestra kept playing, unaware that one of their own was dying.

After the crowd was informed of what had just transpired, the conductor then led the orchestra in Beethoven's Seventh Symphony. The crowd, shocked no doubt, gasped in horror and left the theater. What might have seemed callous to the crowd, though, might have been a tribute in the eyes of the conductor.

If you truly want to see a ghost, hang around for a while after a performance. That's when sightings usually take place.

Science Hall

If you had to pick one place on campus that you thought would be haunted on the basis of looks, you would most likely pick Science Hall. Chances are, it *is* the most haunted place on campus. And it isn't even the original Science Hall. That one burnt down in 1884.

The building has a lot of history. It's the first known building that Frank Lloyd Wright ever worked on and is a National Historic Landmark. The entrance boasts beautiful stained glass and wooden floors that are older than most people alive today.

Another rumor that may or may not be true: A worker was said to be killed during the building of Science Hall. He's now said to roam the maze of halls in the building. Students in certain rooms have witnessed beakers coming off shelves and breaking on the floor. Ghost coming through! Or not?

When the current Science Hall was finished, it became home to the UW Anatomy Department. It's not a stretch to say that the cadavers there sometimes outnumbered the living. That's probably why many believe the ghosts of the cadavers still wander the building. Medical students had twenty-four-hour access to the cadaver lab so they could practice their surgical skills. When they were finished, they got rid of the dissected corpses via a four-story body chute. It's almost impossible not get a mental picture.

The attic of Science Hall is now a storage room where bats still "hang." It's also a place where students found human bones—as late as 1974. It's anyone's guess when the bones took their final "walk" up to the attic...

Camp Randall

Numerous reports of soldier ghosts have been reported here. This shouldn't be surprising given Camp Randall's history.

The camp was used to train Wisconsin troops during the Civil War before sending them off to battle. Something I wasn't aware of: In the spring of 1862, it was also a prison camp for Confederate soldiers. These are the ghosts most often spotted and heard.

These Confederate ghosts are usually in their twenties, and wearing 1800s hairstyles and moustaches. Some of these ghost soldiers wear slings, some stare out windows. One interesting sighting is of a young woman of that time period. She's said to be a stationary figure, head hanging, and looking very "tired." While it may or may not be a nurse, it might be a young woman who accompanied her husband and brother—both prisoners, to Camp Randall. Along the way her husband and children (she brought them with, too) died. At camp, she and her brother became seriously ill with lung fever. Though the woman and her brother did not die here, perhaps she still lingers because of the "good treatment" she received when she was at camp.

Many of the men who trained or were prisoners of Camp Randall never returned home. This was their last earthly stop. The old field house is rumored to be where soldiers underwent surgery. The sounds of men in agony have often been heard there. These ghostly cries have been attributed to soldiers undergoing surgery.

Tunnel Bob of Madison East

Madison East High School, Madison.

Just like UWM, Madison East has a Tunnel Bob. And just like UWM, Madison East's Tunnel Bob is based on a real person that probably existed, and probably lived or existed in the steam tunnels below the school.

Not only is Tunnel Bob talked about on the Internet, in school and out, he's also been featured in *Tower Times*, East Side High School's very-nice-by-anyone's-standards, newsletter. In the April 2007 issue, Tunnel Bob, along with crats (rats of unusual size) were investigated.

Apparently, the tunnels of East, like those under other esteemed schools of Madison, contain things that some of us don't usually

think of on a daily basis. As I read the newsletter—and the article "Tour of East: a look inside," I also learned a little more about another place in East that has been deemed haunted by some of its former students: the theater. The theater, which was renovated in the 1970s, is said to house a ghost. This ghost doesn't have a name or even a gender, but it is said to help the drama department by switching lights on and off. This helpful presences is said to give some students the creeps, but most feel the theater ghost is ready to lend a hand should the need arise. Now back to Bob...

A stairway leads away from the old kitchen. A door then leads to a huge and dusty tunnel. Remnants of a time long gone were found during the investigation, including a Varsity soda can. Apparently Bob, or whoever hung around the tunnels, liked grape soda. Probably needed it to combat the heat produced by the steam lines in the tunnels.

Lest you think the tunnel is a really cool place to hide or hang out for a while, you should be aware that the tunnel is filthy. It's also where old equipment is stored—not a lot of lounging space.

However, in days gone by, someone did indeed try to live in the tunnels. Most likely a homeless person (man), but the staff, no doubt, put an end to his efforts.

Even if the man, in life, didn't live in the tunnels, his ghost is said to remain in spirit in the tunnels of East. Some say they've seen shadows slipping around the corner. Some say they've even seen a homeless man, or a ghost, trying to evade detection in the less traffic-prone areas of the school.

Tunnel Bob may not be the school mascot, but he certainly gives the school a little more spirit.

UW–Rock County

S tudents in the university theater in Janesville have heard doors opening and closing on their own and seen lights going on and off without the aid of human hands.

The sound of "whispering" can also be heard in the theater. Witnesses have heard people "talking" in the theater when no one else was around, and also the sound of doors opening.

Many believe the person responsible for the otherworldly sounds is a former theater instructor or director.

The university is located at 2909 Kellogg Avenue.

University of Wisconsin Madison Alumni Ghost Stories

The stories below are some you will never forget. I can't! If you've ever considered attending the university, you will *definitely* want to attend after reading the "haunting" stories submitted to *On Wisconsin* magazine by alumni.

The following stories in this section are reprinted with permission from the Fall 2006 issue of *On Wisconsin* Magazine (author: John Allen).

Lincoln Statue

Here is a ghost story. A couple of years ago, when I was still an undergraduate in Economics department, a relative of one friend of mine visited him in Madison. She is a 20 years woman from Taiwan and did not speak English. My friend was very busy managing his business on University Ave. So he asked me to show that girl around the campus. So I took this job and brought her entering the campus area. Once we approached to Bascom Hall and I was ready to introduce Lincoln's statue to her, she suddenly looked very scary and asked me to leave that place as soon as possible. I was very frustrated but followed her anyway. She later told me that she saw two more heads behind Lincoln's head. One was an old man and one was relatively young. And they all smiled to her.

I thought that was a joke until several weeks later when the girl had left Madison already. I was reading Badger Herald one day morning and it contains a special edition called 10 most haunted places on campus. It read: "Lincoln Statue was the second haunted place and there buried two males in 18XX."

—*Ying Chan '02*

Bascom Hall

When I was at the UW from 1960-1965, we heard stories about Mr. Bascom. Of course walking on the old floorboards of Bascom Hall, where I took my very first class, always brought squeaks. These were supposed to be the groans and moans of the ghost of Mr. Bascom, directed at us students, because we weren't studying hard enough,

but were out on the Commons sledding, and on Johnson Street burning our bras, and letting our underarm hair grow to perilous lengths. (Not me of course!)

—*Judith Kickland '65*

Music Hall

As a music student (1967-72), I was fortunate enough to participate in a number of Opera productions at Old Music Hall. The great Prof Karlos Moser, director of the Opera, has mentioned lots of creepy things when he had his offices there (doors being locked, yet things moved around...) My own personal experiences were backstage at the Union theatre, when someone would brush up against me, but no one was there. This happened more than once. Very interesting and exciting; always made for a good show...

—*Ramon Gawlitta '72*

I don't know if this is really a ghost story, but it was a little unnerving. A few years ago when I was a freshman at the UW I took a theater painting workshop. I had to make up some missed class time so I volunteered to help my TA paint the set for the upcoming Hansel and Gretel opera in Music Hall. When I got to the hall, my TA was already there. All the doors were locked and I had to knock for some time before she came to answer the door. Apparently, she didn't know the knocking was coming from outside because for a while before I got there she had been hearing strange noises from the balcony, but no one was there. Then after we were painting on the stage for a while, the stereo in the workshop, which is just below the stage, turned on by its self. There was no one else in the building, and the stereo was just a boom box that some one had plugged in and it didn't have a timer or any sort of programming or alarms that could have been set to go off.

—*Rebecca Redmond '05*

North Hall

My experience into the unexplained occurred in North Hall in March of 1983. I was working for campus Police and Security, in addition to pursuing a degree at that time. While routinely patrolling the halls at around 2:45 AM of a very quiet Sunday morning, I stood in utter amazement as a heavy fire door that was at the entryway to the second floor hall opened fully. Naturally, I got into position to take on

whoever was there since at that time of night they had to be up to no good. I got a good view of the hall and landing behind the door too. No practical jokes. No one there. Absolutely nothing. There was no wind that night. So the door should not have moved. No explanation for it at all. I continued down the hall only to be confronted with the certainty that there was something in the hall with me that I could not see but I could sense. I just can't explain the feeling.

It was just knowing with a strange certainty that something was there. And whatever "it" was, was coming in my direction. I had not had time to think on it at all—initially no time to become frightened. There was a gentle draft of air and the temperature around me dropped. It was exactly like walking into the old meat locker at a Wendy's burger place I used to work at. I felt equally certain that "it" was going to make physical contact at any moment.

Needless to say I determined to exit the building quickly. I had thought of getting on my police radio and calling the dispatcher to tell them we had someone in North Hall. I did not depress the microphone button. What was I going to tell them when they asked me to describe "the subject," a perpetrator who could not be seen but only sensed? I had visions of the captain of my shift putting his arm around my shoulders and suggesting I take a few weeks off.

The real draw of this experience is that I had the very same part of the campus to patrol the very next night. The night custodial staffs of our campus buildings, just like daytime department office staffs, can tell you all you want to know about a place. When I routinely asked the crew that had responsibility for that building about it I got an exchange that I quote here verbatim:

Have you guys ever noticed anything strange in North Hall?" (Note that I did not ask any kind of a leading question here.)

"Oh, you've seen the ghost!" replied no less than three of them immediately.

They claimed that they had had regular experiences with a ghost of what they believed was a Political Science professor who had died of a heart attack while working late one Saturday night in the building in 1956, or thereabouts, and who was known to patrol the building in death, as he had done while working late in life so many years ago. I was told his office was on the fourth floor, room 412, and that I must have disturbed him, and that he had followed me down from there as I worked my way down the building checking

doors, only catching up to me when I had lingered to check a book bag left in a classroom. The crew at North Hall had seen this guy regularly, or so they claimed. He would appear walking down the stairwell behind the crew as they left for a night, and he might be seen standing next to a custodian as he wet mopped a floor.

For my part, I determined to repeat exactly what I had done the night before. I entered the building and began my check at precisely the same time as the night before. The crew had left an hour before so I was utterly alone there. I retraced my steps exactly. Only one thing was changed from the night previous: when I rattled the door to room 412 I called out: "It's just Security professor! All's Well! Good Night!"

Needless to say, when I turned to view the heavy fire door on the second floor as I had done the night before, even a scurrying church mouse could have caused me to wet my pants. But nothing happened. I was to be in that building at all hours of the night many times after that but I never had such an experience again. There are many places on the University of Wisconsin-Madison campus I know well that are spooky, but my vote for the most haunted of campus buildings goes to North Hall.

Note: I am fully prepared to sign a written affidavit saying that what I have just told you is the absolute truth as I know it. If nothing else this makes for a good story.

—*Thomas Martin Sobottke '84, MA'89*

Radio Hall

Two things come to mind: Radio Hall, where my office used to be located, always seemed to have something ethereal going on, e.g. an "eyes watching you" kind of feeling. And there's an old water pumping station on Gilman that was turned into an apartment building— apparently there was a fire there sometime in the early-mid 1900's, and a lot of students/former students who have lived there have seen some kind of ghostly thing "fleeing" in the basement hallway...

—*Timothy K. Rusch*

I recently retired from a nearly 3 decade long career with Wisconsin Public Television. One of my duties there was coordinating our office moves. Six or seven years ago, a number of our staff were slated to move into quarters in Radio Hall. Radio Hall has served many departments over the years. Reportedly there's a walk-in

cooler in the basement used to hold the cadavers from Science Hall. WHA Radio used the building for perhaps 50 years. Most recently, it had been occupied for by the staff of I. C. S. (Instructional Communications Systems). Television was moving in now.

Following a lengthy clean-up, painting and carpeting project it was time install office furniture and the partition systems. We began working with those contractors in early August. Things were moving along nicely though I had to come back after-hours and check on the progress of a couple of things. I entered the building and turned on the lights around 10 pm. The building was locked up when I arrived, I was certain that I was the only one there. It was late at night, the air conditioning had shut down, the place was slightly warm and quite silent.

I was standing in the lobby, reviewing the floor plans and decided to head downstairs to check on a couple of things. That's when I felt it. At first, it was a draft, a cool draft on he back of my neck. But the air conditioning had shut down. Then it came again, this time more like someone was there with me, again another cool draft though the AC was still not running. No noises, no voices, just the presence and another cool breeze on the back of my neck.

At that point, I decided the inspection trip to the basement of Radio Hall could wait till tomorrow. It was time to turn off the lights, lock the doors and go home.

Was it Earl Terry, Edgar Gordon or one of the hundreds of Radio Pioneers who labored over consoles, microphones and tape recorders for many years? Or perhaps the soul of someone from the basement cooler?

—Donald Sanford '61

Helen C. White

I received my Ph.D. in English in June 2005, and spent much time at Helen C. White Hall. The administrative assistants who told me about this have retired, but it's about Helen C. White's ghost.

When you wait for the elevator to go up to the English department, you see a portrait of her in a lilac colored mat. That was apparently her favorite color, as she is supposedly wearing a suit of that color in the portrait. Who knows—it looks rather black and white to me. One of the administrative assistants said that on occasion she would get a whiff of lilac out of nowhere, while walking in the hallway. She

claimed it was Helen C. White's ghost walking around. I don't recall having such an experience at all, but what makes this story interesting is that it came from the assistant who was known to smoke like a chimney, so her sense of smell would be much duller than most non-smokers...

—*May Caroline Chan*

Historical Society

When I was a senior (5th year) I worked for a security company as a guard. The company had a contract to provide the guard services for the Wisconsin Historical Society Building. I would usually close the building when I worked. Part of the closing routine was to go through the building to make sure that no students or visitors were still in the building. In addition, I would also have to use a key clock and go around the building to get the key clock punched to show that I had patrolled the building. One evening after clearing the building, while doing my last patrol, I happened to be going through a section of the basement that is not used by the public. As part of that patrol, I use the elevator to get to the basement. I then would turn off the elevator and go through that area, using the stairs to leave. This particular part of the building is pitch black. I was almost done patrolling the area and about to walk up the stairs when the elevator doors opened and then closed, and the elevator then started going up! I froze. The hairs on the back of my neck were standing on end. I went to check the power, and the elevator power was still shut off. Then the elevator came back down and the doors opened and closed again. No one was in the elevator...

—*Matthew Abad '92*

Memorial Library

I'm sure you'll get a few stories about the cages in the Memorial Library stacks. I am creeped out by those--by the idea behind them, that people lock themselves in there in attempt to force productivity. Sometimes they hang sheets over the door so you can't see inside, then you can't tell if anyone is in there until they move or make a noise, which is pretty creepy. Sorry I don't have a specific story, but I'm sure you'll get a few.

—*Luisa Capecchi '06*

I'm not sure if this is what you're looking for, but in the early '80s I used to hide myself in the Memorial Library stacks I believe on Level 3M. There were solo "cages " (mainly for grad students as they had locks on some of the cage doors) illuminated by a single light bulb. Kind of reminded me of the intake cell of the Dane County Jail. Anyway, it sure got spooky in there as midnight approached and things were shutting down. Around that time or shortly thereafter a female student was attacked by the "Axe-Man". On a somewhat related note, my uncle was a Professor in the Medical Microbiology Dept. with his offices in the Service Memorial Institute. There was some funky research going there (he had guinea pigs). The Ag barns also had some pretty wild looking research projects there, too.

—*Jacob Blazkovec '82*

In 1967/1968 I was an assistant to the Western Language Bibliographer at the UW Memorial Library. My job was to identify books on a catalog list to see if they were already among the collection of the UW Library. Often these books would be listed under an editor or another publisher and I had to track them down to make sure that they would not be inadvertently repurchased. I had to go to book shelves throughout the library looking for the books I was assigned to locate. My job often took me to the dimly lighted stacks or "Cutter" collection. The stacks have carrels or study nooks in many parts. Often I was the only person in the immediate area. Frequently, however, I would hear the click of a light going on or off in a carousel booth and there would be no one around. Sometimes I would also find a book or manuscript on a table or carousel booth that had not been there when I came, and I had seen no one in the immediate area. The unexplained phenomena of lights going off/on or finding reading materials on a table where they hadn't been before bothered me at first. After a while, however, I got used to it.

—*K. E. Halverson '69*

Memorial Union

This story is short, in a word: Bus Top (I probably have the spelling wrong, this is the phonetic version). Bus was the barber who held court in the bowels of the Union building by the lake from about 20 BC through approximately 1990 give or take a decade. Actually the truth is he cut hair for over 60 years, most of the time at the Union (I was at So-&-So's

shop up on sumpinorother street for my first year, then I moved to old man whatsits shop till the summer of 25, then I came here). Bus passed away in the nineties and while I have no proof that he haunts his old establishment, I'll bet that if you sneak in, and sit in his old shop, close your eyes and feel the silence, you will, without a doubt, feel a bit of a static charge build up on the hairs of your head and you will perceive on the edge of hearing a faint snip snip.

—Robert Higbee, MS'85

Yes, the rumors have been around for decades, and though I certainly believe "ghosts" exist in some form, I'd never been one who'd put a lot of stock in hauntings. And yet, perhaps because of my stubborn view on the subject, I had an otherworldly experience on campus in 1988, the year I graduated. I spent much of my undergraduate career working for the Wisconsin Union Theatre, the beautiful hall in Memorial Union. The stories were shared with all of the newcomers to the theatre. Several people had died in the theatre over the nearly 50 years it had been open at that point, including some performers. One of the stories dealt with sightings of a ghost on stage after hours. Well, one night, well after a performance had ended, a friend and I had found our way back into the house (don't worry, I was still on duty). The theatre had been a madhouse that night, so we decided to enjoy the peace of the hall in its empty state for a few moments before locking up. The stage was lit with the traditional single light bulb on stage (you never want a theatre to be completely dark, it's bad luck), we were sitting quietly listening to the air moving in the house, when suddenly we were both jarred into hyper-consciousness by a thunderously loud BANG from backstage.

The air on my arms stood straight up, all I could hear was the sound of my heart doing its best to jump from my chest. My friend looked at me and mouthed "WHAT WAS THAT?" I shrugged and was about to suggest a quick departure when our eyes were drawn to the right side of the stage where we both saw something in white move across the stage, stop in the middle for a moment and gaze our over the empty seats, and move to the opposite end where it simply disappeared. We didn't scream, or run, we were too mesmerized. We both reported, over a very large pitcher of beer on the terrace afterwards, a sense of calm that fell over us. Neither of us were scared once we saw the apparition. Our stories were identical, we both saw and felt the same thing. The next day, when I told

then Theatre Operations Manager Francie Cohen what we'd seen, she simply shrugged her shoulders and calmly said, "Oh, you saw the ghost, he's the one I told you about, he's been around forever." And to this day, though I've never had another experience like this, I tell this story fondly for it's part of the mystique of the campus that I love.

—Michael Harryman, '88

Red Gym

Your upcoming unearthing of ghosts on campus reminds me of the eponymously nicknamed Red Gym, now probably more gloriously rechristened....

It was the early 1970s and the Red Gym, AKA the Armory, had been "firebombed" a year or so earlier and stood boarded up and forlorn. The damage done to it was not really noticeable from the outside except for the plywood covering the windows on its tower. The real damage was done by whoever went in afterward, presumably the firefighters, and hosed it down mightily as well as covered its interior with chemical foam. Tightly boarding up the windows and leaving the mess in situ made for a nice stew over the ensuing months.

Across Langdon Street from the mess squatted the University Library, home to the University Archives, where Frank Cook presided with great benevolence. (If he's still around, he could name names, ghost-wise, for you, I'm sure.) Frank was, as all archivists are, in charge of collecting any University-related droppings and preserving them for posterity. The ground-floor tower of the Red Gym had been, prior to The Incident, the office of a University athletic coach, who had amassed a goodly stock of records in it. Frank was asked if the University Archives could retrieve these. Like a good manager, Frank passed this to his subordinate, who passed it to his subordinate. Me.

So on a steamy summer day, armed with two loads of flattened field boxes, I took the keys to said office to collect papers. I had been warned that there was only a single light bulb depending from the center of the ceiling (what was left of it) that worked. The tricky part was getting to the light bulb to switch it on, since there was a gaping hole in the center of the blitzed room where an extra-large safe had found it prudent to descend to the lower levels of the building after the wooden floor got soaked. The room was pitch-dark, full of

moldering chaos, and stank mightily. A hasmat suit and flashlight would have come in handy, but I'd neglected to bring either.

The watery light down the hallway afforded some view of the office's interior, which, like the tower, was roughly round. In the gloom at the far side of this hellhole loomed what looked like a small army of glinting amputees, frozen in mid-activity. I dropped the load of boxes into the congealing mass at my feet and, feeling for the wall, edged around the gaping hole, groping in the dark at peeling bits of wallpaper, broken glass frames, and overturned file cabinets.

By the time I had crept around to the far end of the room, I was sweating freely. The room had no air, and the chemicals in it, coupled with the reek of formaldehyde from dozens of large broken specimen bottles (oh, yes, forgot to mention that the room next to the coach's office had been some sort of lab storage area, also trashed beyond recognition....some of the escaped squodgy bits from the jars oozed quietly around the floor...) made breathing impossible. And now I was standing next to the horde of human forms, some of whom were lying at my feet in grotesque postures of....

Oh, bollocks. It was the deposed coach's collection of oversized sports trophies, now mangled into scrap metal, staring back at me vacantly, some with severed limbs outstretched in former glory, others in poses of well-muscled flight minus a leg or two. If I'd known it was in there, I would have snatched the coach's starter pistol from the upturned desk drawer and fired freely into the lot of them.

But they proved helpful in their darkest hour, those mannequins of triumphant athletic might. I seized the largest one I could reach and, leaning over the chasm caused by the sinking safe, snagged the elusively dangling light cord with the statue's one remaining arm. The popping light from the 40-watt bulb did little to decrease the gloom, but it brought the room's demands into plainer view. Dollops of chemical foam, frozen into place drooped over everything, "everything" being case after case of mangled file drawers, desks, and scattered congealing paper mounds. I fought my way back to the doorway and gulped in the fresh air. It would take weeks to clean this out.

That summer was the hottest Madison had endured in years. And it ultimately took months, not weeks, to clean out that round room. I still wonder who that coach was. But I remember the long, slow sigh behind me as I left the room for the last time....

—Anonymous

Science Hall

If "Science Hall" is the building on the corner of university and north charter (next to the physics bldg) then I can assure you that ghosts roam (or at least , roamed) freely on the top floor during the nocturnal hours. I did my PhD up there in 1970-73. I used to work late in the lab, and the presence of unseen others was standard stuff. They were not scary in the least—and in a way reassuring (yesss, your research will come out alright). In the summer of '70 there was a mild disturbance one night, which was heard 26 miles away, and which decimated much of the building I worked in. Fortunately my thesis worked survived. A few weeks before the blast, one of the students discovered an ancient attic room at the top of the building. Just walking in there was like going back a hundred years; the old glassware, balances, pharmacy prescriptions from the 1800s. There was also a lot of dust. Unfortunately, the explosion destroyed the old attic. I very much regretted no longer having that time machine around when I got tired of work.

—*Eric M. Gordon PhD'73*

My mother, Shirley Stillpass Wagner '47, was in the first class of Occupational Therapy. She said that they had to dissect the cadavers in the basement of Science Hall, as part of their classwork. She said that those sessions were always frightening because of the ghosts that were in the building and from the dead that they worked on.

—*Linda Wagner Berman '73, MS '86*

Camp Randall

I started dating a Physics Graduate student in the Spring of 2000. Often I would study with him in his office late into the night on the 3rd floor of the Physics Building—Sterling Hall. One night I was walking to the women's restroom on the 3rd floor and in the far corner of the hallway saw an injured Confederate solder. He appeared to be a young man— early, perhaps mid 20s; 5 feet 8 to 10 inches tall; dark brown hair and a long pointy mustache. He wore a Confederate gray shirt and pants and a cap which appear too big for him. His right arm was in a white swath sling. He was looking out the window that was pointing South. (I know because I checked the layout of the building). The first time I saw him, I ran back to

my boyfriend's (now husband's) office and told him he had to walk me to the restroom. The apparition was gone when we returned.

A few weeks later, the same scenario occurred except that he was guarding/standing in front of the women's restroom and said, "Excuse me, Ma'am, when do you think we'll be allowed home?"

I'm no historian, but I believe that Camp Randall was a Civil War detainment camp.

—Anonymous

I have a unique point of view for the UW-Madison campus. Since the early 1940s a member of our family has attended the Madison Campus. My father was a associate professor in engineering during the 1970s-80s and we did/still live in the Madison area (excluding myself of course). Since I was the son of a professor I had the opportunity to use the campus as my playground growing up. There are several stories of ghosts on campus that I can remember, two come to mind. The old Camp Randall site was used for military training for Wisconsinites for the Civil War. It has been rumored that a surgical site/hospital was placed where the old field house is now. Wounded soldiers from the battles were transported back and attended to on this site for recovery. Many soldiers never left this site alive. It has been said that some sounds have been heard of screaming men near the field house. Those screams were attributed to the surgeons procedures on the dying men.

Another memorial one involves the extensive tunnel system under the Madison campus. Some say that you can walk from one end of campus to the other and never have to come above ground. I know personally that this is true of most buildings near and on Bascom hill. The story goes that a hippie/vagrant lives in the underground system. The university actually knows about this person and due fully employs him to maintain the sub-tunnel system by changing out light bulbs and reporting problems. I have never seen this man, but was assured that he existed.

Over the many years hanging out at the University you get to know all of the colorful characters that have attached themselves to this campus. UW-Madison does have a blend of people from all eras in its history dead and alive. All you have to do is look and they are there in the shadow of the Library Mall, Bascom Hill, Lincoln's Face. Someday maybe someone will write about them.

—Jacob Brown '96

Vilas Hall

In 1986 or thereabouts, the Daily Cardinal was just beginning to install desktop publishing. One of the students went down the hall into the UW Type Lab and asked if anyone knew what this meant. The database had typed out "ORV" in xxx's on a sheet of paper. Orv Larson, was the legendary Daily Cardinal printer who had died the winter before. Eerie but true. Orv worked 3rd shift. Used to bring back beer from the Black Bear Lounge. Cough when he pulled open the pop top. If people hear an occasional cough in the wee hours of the night in Vilas Hall, it might be Orv, getting ready to sip one of Wisconsin's finest products.

—*Dave Newman*

Warehouse

I worked in the UW Warehouse (next to the Kohl Center) for DoIT Logistics from March of 1997 until December of 2002. My co-workers and I saw and heard what I believe to be a ghost, many times over the years. I even have a photo on my desk of a picture taken of it!

The first time I experienced this, I was alone working in the warehouse when there was loud banging on the other side of a large metal overhead door. I was in a security locked area and would not open the door until someone would identify themselves. I kept asking 'who is there?' But no one would answer. The banging continued for several minutes. I complained later to the warehouse manager who insisted that it was not him and was concerned about who was in the back warehouse area. He was also concerned for my safety since I often worked alone, so he installed a large mirror above the door so that if anyone was knocking on the door or pounding on the metal overhead door I would be able to look up through an open area and see the entire wall. Several times later the banging would happen again and I could plainly see in the mirror that no one was there.

Another time I was in the stacks of computers taking inventory when a movement caught my eye. I looked up to see a man walking several aisles away and disappear behind a stake of boxes. There was only one entrance that people could come into and all the rest of the doors were kept locked. I called out to the person asking if they needed help and went around to the aisle where I had seen him walk and there was no one there.

Over the years I saw and heard this man several other times. He had reddish hair and a beard and always was wearing the same shirt, blue jeans and tan work shoes. One of my co-workers that covered my shift one day told me that he had seen the man also and now was a believer too!

The photo I have was taken by a co-worker. He brought in his camera one day to take pictures of the warehouse and the staff. When he got all the pictures developed, all of them came out fine except for the one of me. You can see the light that was on my desk but there is a large orange glow in the shape of a person standing right next to wear I was sitting.

I was told, and don't know if it is true, that a man died in that area many years ago when he was crushed by a train on the tracks that use to run through the area that is now enclosed and part of the warehouse. Thanks for letting me share my story!

—*Martha Querin-Schultz*

Liz Waters

When I was chosen president of Elizabeth Waters Hall by a vote of the residents in my junior year, I lived in the president's suite with my roommate. The "suite" was a slightly larger double room in the center section of the dorm above the front door entrance to the dorm. When we moved in, we heard the suite was haunted, and that you could hear the moaning and groaning of ghosts from years past.

At that time no men were allowed in the dorm at any time, except for invited guests for Sunday Dinner only. (In fact whenever repairs of some kind had to be made on one of the floors of one of the 5 houses of the dorm, the level or floor had to be cleared of all women residents, before the repairmen were allowed in.) Sunday dinner was always a sit-down served meal, not a cafeteria line. All women had to wear skirts, not long pants or shorts. Everyone, as a group from each dinner table, had to, stop at the Housemother's table, where the Housefellows also sat (Women graduate students that counseled students and lived in the five halls of the dormitory). Students and their friends had to stop at the table for conversation, and introduce either themselves, if they were alone, or their dinner companion, whether it was a female friend or visitor, or a male friend. If this was not done, the Housemother would walk around to each table to say hello, and be introduced to our visitors.

Because, no men were ever allowed in the dorm, except for Sunday dinner, if you had a date and wanted to say good night with a kiss, you had to do it out in front of the main doors to the dormitory, standing on the concrete platform at the front of the dorm. This lead to the production of some moans and groans, possibly from "standing so long on the concrete," or due to some other things! Of course, because our room, with windows often open, was right above that platform, we heard much of this commotion. Since there was curfew at, I believe, 10:00 or 10:30 pm on weeknights and 12:00 midnight on weekends, and the dorm housed 500 young women, there were usually quite a few couples out in front of the dorm saying goodnight right up to closing time. Of course my roommate and I never explained the situation to anyone, we just passed along the story of the moaning and groaning of ghosts that could be heard in the President's suite at Liz Waters Hall. Thank you for the opportunity to relate this information to you. It was fun remembering after all these years! Have a special day! On Wisconsin!

—Judith (Judy) A. Kickland

Kronshage

I attended UW Madison from 1992-1996 and heard quite a few ghost stories. I lived in Kronshage Hall (Showerman house) my first year and remember a story that supposedly happened to one of the residents there that year. If I recall, the story freaked out the people in the dorm-including myself. Here is what I remember. A young man was living in the first floor of the dorm. I guess he had brought a glass of water (or some beverage—I don't remember) from the dining hall and left it on his dresser before he went to bed. (His roommate was away for the weekend). Apparently he woke up to a strange sound like someone had thrown something across the room. When he turned on the light, the glass which he had left on the dresser was now in front of the door unbroken. I remember him saying he swears he did not move it.

I also remember hearing reports from other residents (men and women) that during the night, they would see a dark shadowy figure at the end of the hallway of the second floor of that same dorm. I never encountered anything out of the ordinary at this particular dorm...However when I moved out to an apartment at 2110 Old University Avenue, I did encounter some unexplained incidents. I

interned for a morning show at one of the television stations and got up fairly early. Early one morning, when I opened my bedroom door to go get some breakfast, I am positive I saw a young woman sitting on our couch and looking towards the window in the living room. At first I thought it was my roommate, but the girl was very blonde and my roommate was a brunette. I assumed it probably was a friend of hers that had spent the night, so I turned on the living room light, and the figure disappeared. Needless to say it freaked me out.

When I told my roommate about what I had seen she told me that she on more than one occasion had heard voices within the apartment. I guess once when she was alone and studying she heard a loud laugh coming from my bedroom. She thought I was home and reading something funny. About ten minutes later I came home from class. The look on her face when she saw me come in was priceless. I had not been home all day, so she couldn't explain who it was she heard. I cautiously opened my bedroom in case an intruder or something, but no one was in there. I can't explain what I saw, or what she heard, but it freaked both of us out. Anyway, those are my ghost stories. I don't know if you can use them, but it was fun (and a little freaky) remembering them.

—*Brenda Velasco '96*

Turner

August 1958. Age 28, married, pretty much past earlier fraternity foolishness. Attending Graduate classes. Home weekends to mow lawn, etc. Living in Turner House. After lunch, we routinely walked to library to study until 4 then back to Turner to swim, relax, dine, play Intramural Softball, etc. till dark. Then study until ten and head for the Hasty Tasty for a couple of beers and a hamburger. Point I am making is that I was more-or-less past my earlier "prankster", college days.

My roommate, colleague and buddy, Carl Reck, and I regularly took the lake path from Turner Hall to the library and back each afternoon. At that time, a portion of this shoreline path went through a patch of natural woods and thicket close to the water. One afternoon, while the trip to the Union and library was uneventful, the trip home was a real shocker. The wind had been from the southwest both to and from the library.

We smelled nothing peculiar on the way to the library but, on the way back, the unmistakable strong stench of something large, dead and rotting wafted from that thicket. It was so strong that we both stopped in our tracks when it hit us. Surprised that we hadn't smelled it a few hours earlier as we passed by, we decided to investigate.

It was a badly bloated, corpse in a skirt and blouse. It was on its back. The face was almost gone and was covered with a mass of maggots and crawling flies. We hurried to report it. When we came back to point it out, it was gone without a trace. That is, there was no depression in the ferns and undercover where body had lain. There were no left-over maggots or swarming flies on the ground. There was not a hint of dead animal odor; no remaining stench. No signs that a body had been carried out and away. No footprints, broken ferns, turned up leave—nothing. No currently missing co-ed. Nothing. The body was gone without a trace. Case was never solved. Actually, maybe never even recorded because there was absolutely no evidence that we were telling the truth. The campus police probably just gritted their teeth and walked away from what they considered to be just another annoying frat joke. How could there be no smell or other evidence that a rotting body had been there minutes earlier? Amazing! The only evidence was probably the dismay and honest confusion shown on our faces. This must have been sufficient to save us from being written up for pulling a pointless juvenile prank. Easy to see how the police could come to that conclusion but, we were there! There really was a stinking body covered with flies and maggots. How could it completely disappear in a matter of minutes? Frat fun? If so, how was it pulled off leaving no evidence? A ghost? An apparition? That seems only slightly more believable. But, if so, for what purpose? What was the message? Why us and what for?

—Don Forbes MS'60

Sellery

When I was living in the dorms in 1987, a group of adventurers students from Sellery B, 3rd floor ELY house, traveled in the steam tunnels below campus on a routine basis. One night, in a tunnel below Bascom Hill, we spotted another person following us about 30-40 feet back, always at the edge of our visibility. When we stopped, the other person stopped and when we walked towards them they moved away. After calling out a few times to see who it was, we decided to lay a trap at

the next turn. We left our friend Jim hiding behind the main steam pipe and the rest of us proceeded down the tunnel. When we had traveled a short distance we heard Jim call out "got'ch ya!" and then "Holy S$#@". He came running towards us yelling "RUN LIKE HELL!" We all took off at best speed and ran to the nearest exit just to the west of the hill. When Jim came out of the tunnel he was white as a ghost and pretty shaken up. He would not tell us anything until we got back to the dorm. After a few shots of rum, he told us that he saw what looked like another student come around the corner of the tunnel and when he jumped out and tried to grab him his hand went right through the arm. From that night on Jim refused to go back to the steam tunnels. We went back a few more times but never saw the "student" again. After a while we all felt like something bad was going to happen when we explored the tunnels and decided to find other things to do.

—Paul Gilmartin '90

Witte

I surely have a UW ghost story! My roommate Ted Dootson and I lived in 854 Witte B in 1989-90. One night we both swear to seeing the same ghost in our room. Our whole floor likely remembers this night! It was the outline of a young Asian girl. First she hovered over Ted vertically when I first noticed her and woke him up. He became startled & she moved to a sitting position on our dorm refrigerator. We both saw the same girl & saw her in our room for a few minutes in these positions. I know for a fact that year, our freshman year at UW, these 2 Hodags saw a ghost in 854 B. She was nice and unconcerned for the most part & we never saw her again. From then on I have been a true believer in ghosts—an added benefit to the many from my time at Madison!

—Chris Winkler '93

Chi Psi

I know of a few ghost stories about the Chi Psi Lodge on Iota Court in Madison. The building was built between 1911-1913, and has had many people living there since then. I lived there for my Junior and Senior year (class of 2001), and didn't see anything myself, but I heard all of the stories. The most prominent is one of a brother that was at the Lodge by himself at night, and was wandering around trying to find anyone to hang out with. As he walked by one of the bathrooms, he spotted someone in his peripheral vision washing

their hands at the sink, but walked by and just said a passing "hey". After checking on a few rooms near the bathroom to see if anyone was home, he returned to the bathroom to see who that was he saw, and nobody was there but the water was still running. He didn't hear or see anyone leave, which he should have since he was only 10 feet from the bathroom at most, but still nothing was there to indicate someone else other than the running water. He says he checked the stalls and everything and saw nobody. He says he turned the water off and returned to his room for the rest of the night, wondering if he did just see what he saw. This story I heard first hand from the brother that experienced it, so I can't believe that it was changed or embellished over years of story telling.

Another older story (and therefore possibly suspect) involves the house mother suite in the basement of the Lodge, of which nobody was living in for a while since the lodge didn't have a house mother. But the story goes that a brother, who was down in the kitchen cooking at the time saw an older lady come through the exterior door, take a right and pass through the wall into the house mother suite. Despite the fact that he was considerably spooked by this, he later found out that the suite's door, which was down in the kitchen at the time, used to be where the ghost passed through the wall. The ghost was later attributed to Maggie, a house mother that lived in the lodge for the first 30 years it was there and died in the suite in the 1940's sometime. This story was one that was passed down from bother to brother, so how much embellishment there is, I don't know, but this is the way I heard it.

There are other stories about doors closing by themselves and other strange sounds coming from the old lodge, and some rooms being haunted more than others, but nothing like the stories above. Also, I know these stories don't involve a university building, but Langdon Street and its surroundings is as much as campus as anything else. Hope these stories help some.

—*Chris Fleming, '01*

Theta Delta Chi

Because this is officially off campus don't know if it counts but 144 Langdon Street (located actually "down" from Langdon off Lake Mendota) is the Theta Delta Chi UW-Madison fraternity standing in an ancient old Madison home. I was a member from 1990 until I graduated from UW in Dec '93.

The story goes that a young female fell to her death down the back stairways years ago (apparently this is a true/confirmed story; not sure of the era of her death)….the vibe around that back hallway stairway is very odd….members of the fraternity whose beds faced up against this wall (like me) would wake up in our sleep banging our arms/hands against the wall many times….

Members who were in the house alone (e.g., around thanksgiving or a holiday when everyone was gone) would tell stories of being scared to hell by hearing running footsteps all around the back stairway to the attic…..NOBODY else was in the house upon searching and looking everywhere….two good friends of mine had this happen….they were CONVINCED someone else was there so they took off running after the sounds but found nobody…..

On occasion in a small vestibule off to the side of the stairway (which use to be the house telephone "booth") an old time phone would ring…..there was/is NO phone connected or even located in this small vestibule anymore….all of us have heard the phone ringing…

The stairway led to a 4th floor attic where there was a work out room…..several different people (including me) had been there working out (w/head phones on) when off to the side there was an intense and real sensation of someone standing there watching you! I remember literally throwing off my ear phones and jumping up from the workout bench to find no one there…….although I continued to work out there in the future other members were spooked enough not to go back up there….

Perhaps among the scariest and most mysterious is an incident that I witnessed…..a few of us were in the house close to one of the aforementioned holidays…the back stairways lead to the basement where the house kitchen/cook area was….to the side of the kitchen is a storage room for food, boxes, freezers etc…..one of the members called down to me and a couple others…..we came down to find that the door to this side room was completed blocked by something…..we pushed as hard as we could for a long time and could only get it to open a few inches…..standing there, right up against the door was one of the huge and heavy old freezers of that back storage room…..

Upon getting more help when more house members were around we finally were able to push the door and freezer back enough to be able to squeeze into this storage room to see who/what was in there and who had done this…..there was nobody in there….how then

did this freezer get pushed up against a door? A room w/o only one way/door out (which was the door it was blocking). WHO could be strong enough to this?

We believed (and still do) that the ghost of this girl who fell to her death in the back stairways was (and is) responsible for all of this.

—*Erik Farmer '93*

Delta Delta Delta

The Delta Delta Delta sorority on Langdon (whatever house it was in the early 90's) is haunted by a former House Mother. She only spooks the old sections of the house, not the new additions. I pulled an all-nighter there while my study partner (and the rest of the sorority—I was the only one up with very few lights on) slept and did not enjoy all the creaking and noises around me one bit. The combination of the sounds with caffeine, exhaustion and by this time total paranoia was too great. I finally went to the basement of all places where she didn't lurk and was able to study. She has a name but I can't remember it. Call a Tri-Delta house and I'm sure you'll get more of the story.

—*Paul Buzzell '93*

Compass Theatre

There were two rather innocent ghosts in the old Compass Theatre back in the summer of 1971. I encountered their heavy breathing and occasional moanings late at night after rehearsals of the play "Little Mary Sunshine." I sang the part of Captain Big Jim Warrington and would frequently hang around long after everyone else had gone home to practice. Once the theatre was completely cleared out (except for me), the sounds would begin. Once started, the sounds increased in intensity until, quite abruptly, they would stop. I would search the building from top to bottom, but never found anyone. On more than one occasion, I would invite one or two other cast members to stay behind with me, but nothing ever happened until I was completely alone. Apparently, these two ghosts were performing only for my benefit.

—*John A. Robinson MFA'72*

Mickey's Dairy Bar

This story involves a favorite eatery near Camp R. stadium called Mickey's dairy bar. For the duration of the time I went there (82

through 89) there was an unfinished mural painted on the right hand wall which I designate in my memory banks as "The Road To Oslo" due to a little sign in the painting which bore this inscription. The sign was next to a rough path, and on the path there was a lonely, dare I say ghostly figure, with his back turned to us walking down a misty road, walking stick in hand. Why had the mural sat unfinished all of those years? Itinerant painter who mysteriously disappeared? Love affair gone sour? I had reason to visit Madison again in the early nineties and I went back to the place (best milk shakes this side of the Mississippi) and to my dismay found them redecorating and painting over the mural. As I sit here and record these events, I can't help but think of the fellow trapped under that layer of beige paint, haunting the wall with his frozen steps.

—*Robert Higbee MS'85*

Madison Researchers Into The Paranormal

Some members of the MRIP team. From left to right: Amanda Hickey, Patrick Denney, Heather Mertz, Gary Westerlund, Jessica Zeier, Wayne Hackler, Abe Vaccaro. Not pictured: Evie Hackler, Abbie Tippit.

I recently sat down with Wayne Hackler of the paranormal investigative organization, Madison Researchers into the Paranormal, or MRIP. One thing that makes this Madison-based organization stand out is how much of a team they really are. The group makes decisions collectively. There is no one person who makes the decisions alone.

I asked Hackler how the group came into being. "It was begun because there was a need for a full-time organization in the area… Networking was key to bringing the group together. All members are like-minded when it comes to serious research. Each is different in their degree of skepticism," he says.

MRIP has been together more than a year and a half as a group.

If someone wants to have MRIP research a possible haunting, they usually contact the group by e-mail initially. (It's confidential. The next step is to fill out an extensive questionnaire. This usually weeds out thrill seekers.) The application is reviewed, and a decision is made to follow up. First MRIP offers possible explanations for the paranormal experience, along with guidance and advice beforehand. If no explanation works, the process continues from there.

In 1991, Hackler didn't have a network system. He had to learn by trial and error. "I'm just inquisitive by nature," he says of his desire to research the paranormal." Around that time, he had a very personal experience with a ghost, but no real organization to connect with. He continued his research on his own as he moved all around the country.

Hackler says his wife, Evie, also in the group, might think he's "kooky," but they got together anyway and she's been very supportive. Her skepticism is a healthy balance to his belief in things outside what others may think of as normal.

When it comes to ghosts, "Everyone has had an experience or wants one," Hackler says.

The MRIP team has fun, but every investigation is taken very seriously. The group has a picnic each year, group outings, and they even get together at members' homes for wine and snacks; this group is very close-knit.

Hackler has experienced unexplained bruises and scratches when he's been at different locations doing investigations. Some might argue he's clumsy or that he walked up against something or scraped himself. To make sure this isn't the case, a videotape is always running during investigations.

Members of MRIP specialize in different areas. Hackler was a history major in college; Abbie Tippit is an EVP specialist, another member is a technical guru… This is very important because the team considers multiple sources of evidence in each case. They believe that evidence must be able to stand as a "three-legged stool" to support a belief that a house or area is haunted. Hackler and the others in the group prefer a preponderance of evidence when it comes to deciding whether a home, business, or elsewhere is haunted.

"We look at things a little differently than a lot of groups," he says. MRIP wants its research to provide evidence that can stand up to scrutiny, so the veracity can't be questioned. MRIP goes one step

further; they try to see if the "condition" of the haunting can be duplicated and they also interview witnesses separately.

Think you have ghost in your home or business? Contact MRIP. The group loves to travel and investigate Madison and just about anywhere else. They thrive on learning and trying to find answers.

Every case goes before a research team. The background is investigated and questions are asked. Why did the experience occur? Where? These and other questions need to be asked—they are of the utmost importance in gaining an understanding of the case. Urban legends are also investigated.

Ever wonder why some places are "haunted" while others aren't? Hackler says, "Emotional imprints can explain why some places are particularly prone to hauntings." For example, in life, if a person enjoyed sitting at a bar, he or she might return after they expire. This might explain why so many bars and taverns in Wisconsin seem to be haunted.

"There are three camps of people," says Hackler. "There are the hardcore skeptics who won't believe anything under any circumstances. Then there are those who believe anything and everything is paranormal. Finally, the biggest group is a mixture of the two groups. These people believe with a dose of skepticism and also possibility."

Orbs are a topic Hackler and the others in MRIP have mixed feelings about. From a physics standpoint, a sphere is the most energy-efficient way for energy to travel. On the other hand, sometimes there are strange-shaped orbs, shadows, etc. that defy a logical explanation.

Hackler says paranormal investigative groups are, "the bastard child of conventional science." In decades past, the government funded research that dealt with the paranormal realm. Now there's no funding involved and this has served to discredit the field.

As more people have access to better equipment, etc., Hackler sees a greater acceptance of paranormal research.

"Anyone can investigate the paranormal," he says. "There are a few things you should do; one is don't go investigating alone. Not just for the safety reasons, but because it's easier to verify claims [if there is more than one person]."

Hackler recalls one case that was claim heavy on one end and weak on another. MRIP was called to investigate a allegation of demons in a home. He remembers the family, a husband, wife, and teenage son, as being very nice people.

The team got to the house and interviewed the husband, wife, and son separately. While they were being interviewed, Hackler was also mentally taking notes. The family members were fundamental Christians. While the husband and wife detailed their experiences, the son said he hadn't experienced anything. The problem? The couple was too religiously zealous to view any of their experiences objectively. Also, the house was an electromagnetic nightmare. Hackler remembers there being a lot of electronics in the house, which meant strong electromagnetic activity. Research has shown this is can be linked to hallucinations and paranoia.

After reviewing the facts, MRIP told the couple they couldn't help them; they should speak to their pastor.

There are those who believe in ghosts and those who don't. Hackler believes how you were brought up and how your belief system is instilled in you is the determining factor in whether you believe in ghosts or not.

"Ghost hunting is not like it is portrayed on TV," says Hackler. "Going through evidence is laborious, but also exciting when you can't explain the evidence away."

He firmly believes that all paranormal stories have some element of truth in them. Usually a story will start with a grain of truth, but through time and retelling, the story snowballs.

MRIP holds monthly meetings, training sessions, and preparations for upcoming cases. Every case is dependent on the schedules of members; their investigations are not funded by anyone other than themselves.

Hackler says there is a difference in attitudes toward ghosts and hauntings. "In the south, ghosts are a matter of pride. In the north, ghosts aren't as acceptable."

Another member of MRIP, Gary Westerlund, has been investigating and forming groups for forty years. Some of the groups he's formed or worked with include Arizona Paranormal Investigation, which is still running, and Hawaii Paranormal Investigations. He's currently with Madison Researchers Into The Paranormal. A college business grad, ex-deputy sheriff, and church leader, Westerlund has investigated over 800 inquiries, been on local, public, and private TV programs, and has been on radio. He's also developed many programs for investigations and has been an advisor to some film studios and writers.

Tippit is the team's EVP specialist. She, Hackler, and Westerlund have graciously answered a few questions about MRIP and themselves.

Q & A with Wayne Hackler, Abbie Tippit, and Gary Westerlund of MRIP

Q: First of all, can you tell me what you'd like everyone to know about Madison Researchers Into The Paranormal?

Wayne Hackler: We all have varied backgrounds and life experiences, but the one thing we all have in common is our passion for the paranormal, and in particular, ghosts and hauntings. Our desire to learn more about the subject through investigation and research will hopefully help propel this field of study further.

Gary Westerlund: Madison Researchers are a fairly new team of people who have had experiences or want some. We are looking for answers regarding the paranormal and all are dedicated to the same case and are willing to be skeptical and scientific as well as open-minded. We are all just your average person next door.

Q: Why do you believe ghosts interact with the world of the living?

Wayne Hackler: I don't think that all of them can, as the prevailing theories break ghosts and hauntings down into several categories. The reasoning why could be as simple as saying, "hello, I'm here," to wanting something done that they were unable to do during their lifetime. As far as physical interaction with our world, this is something that greatly fascinates me. It is a very rare occurrence, prevailing theory being that it takes a large energy expenditure to manipulate the environment.

Gary Westerlund: Ghosts are thought to be just people passed on. They may be looking for answers about their current status, not knowing they are dead, looking for help, or they just like where they are and want to share the same places with us and want us to know they are around.

Abbie Tippit: There are so many theories on why spirits interact with the living. Many believe that there is unfinished business (waiting for the one lost love to return, guilt for something he/she had done wrong while alive, or a wrongful death that should be justified). Other theories include watching over a loved one, attachment to a person, place, or thing, or, on the extreme of the scale, the spirit doesn't believe that he/she is dead. These are all theories and speculation. There is no one exact reason for ghosts to stay around.

Q: What are some of the reasons people contact your group?

Wayne Hackler: Many people just want reassurance that they're not crazy or imagining things. If there is a normal, physical explanation for what they have experienced, we try to provide them that.

Abbie Tippit: Mainly, people are scared of the things they cannot see. Groups like ours are called to help answer the difficult questions and reassure the client that he/she is not crazy.

Q: What types of equipment do you and your team use?

Wayne Hackler: We use still cameras (digital and film), video cameras, night vision cameras, various temperature sensing devices and hygrometers, audio recorders (digital and analog), various EMF measuring devices, motion detectors, infrared spotlights—pretty much anything that we can think of that can serve a purpose and hopefully increase our knowledge.

Gary Westerlund: We use digital cameras, film cameras, EMF meters as well as natural meters that detect changes in magnetic forces, thermometers—digital and regular, dowsing rods, voice recording equipment, 2-way radios, motion sensors, computers, infrared lights and much more.

Abbie Tippit: We use film/digital cameras, video cameras, digital recorders, EMF detectors, flash lights, thermometers, and the list goes on. We also experiment with other different types of equipment.

Q: What three ghost "hunting" items do you think are indispensable to the amateur ghost investigator?

Wayne Hackler: Some things that are indispensable to ghost hunters are common sense and critical thinking skills. All the gadgets in the world will not make you a competent investigator without these two traits. As far as equipment, at the bare minimum a camera and an audio recorder should be used.

Gary Westerlund: Camera, EMF meter, and a recorder.

Abbie Tippit: The bare essentials would be common sense, a partner, and a flashlight. I also highly recommend a cell phone in case of an emergency.

Q: What do you and your team members consider a positive indication of a ghostly encounter or haunting?

Wayne Hackler: We have to look at all the evidence collected (photos, video, audio, and environmental measurements) in conjunction with the history of the location, anecdotal evidence, and investigator impressions. The more items that support each other, the better. We try to recreate reported phenomena and anomalies captured by us. If we are unable to do this, it helps to lend more credence to the possibility of a haunting.

Gary Westerlund: Actual pictures that cannot be explained; actually seeing them as a couple or team, and physical contact.

Abbie Tippit: Corroborating evidence. It's important to have evidence that backs up other evidence. The more evidence you have, the least likely it can be questioned.

Q: What prompted your lifelong passion of the paranormal?

Wayne Hackler: When I was growing up in West Virginia, ghosts and hauntings were accepted as real by most everyone I knew. My family has always had experiences with the paranormal, but it wasn't until I got older and had an experience while I was in the Army that I wanted to know the why and how of ghosts and hauntings.

Gary Westerlund: My grandmother told us of a very strange and unexplainable mass murder of their neighborhood back in 1919 where a whole family was chopped up. It happened after a fresh snow…no tracks and all doors and windows were locked. The way they died, suicide was not possible. From that point on, about age seven, I became very interested and did some research off and on 'til about 20. Then I really dug into it as people started telling their stories to me, many I had never met.

Abbie Tippit: I was raised in the South and people are generally more opened to discussing matters of the paranormal. I grew up hearing stories from friends and relatives and experiencing my own encounters.

Q: Have you had an experience in the Madison area that still makes you shake your head, or left you feeling lucky you escaped unscathed?

Wayne Hackler: I was doing a preliminary survey of a purportedly haunted outdoor location in broad daylight one day in Madison, and I had an overwhelming feeling that I wasn't wanted there and that it would be in my best interest to leave post haste. There was no one around at the time, just me. It was one of the creepiest feelings I've ever had. I left quickly, but the team returned the next day to the site.

Gary Westerlund: No.

Abbie Tippit: Not really.

Q: Do you have a "dream" ghost or location you would like to investigate someday?

Wayne Hackler: That's a tough one. Any place that is truly haunted would be a dream, as opposed to purportedly haunted places that are hyped up by the media and over commercialized.

Gary Westerlund: There are so many places, it is very difficult to say. So many have become so commercialized…but it would have to have an extreme history of paranormal activity and I would be allowed total access to all areas of the place. So many places have areas you can't see for whatever reason. If I could travel to do this I would. Some of the now popular TV shows have very lucky teams as they have all their time and equipment and travel paid for. I'd jump at the chance to quit my job and just ghost hunt.

Abbie Tippit: There are so many that it would be hard to pick. I would like to go somewhere that is unique and has not been investigated before.

Q: Are the ghosts we see on TV and at the theater an accurate portrayal of ghosts that you and your team encounter?

Wayne Hackler: Through the miracles of editing, reality paranormal shows have done us a great disservice. It is not as exciting as portrayed and not every location is haunted in my opinion. Also, even though I personally believe in the existence of Demons and demonic activity, I don't believe it's as prevalent as some would like us to believe. Movies have shown ghosts to be dangerous and vengeful and in my experience 99% of the time this is not the case.

Gary Westerlund: No, Hollywood really distorts ghosts so that ghost hunting, etc., seem more exciting...

Abbie Tippit: I don't believe so. In my own experiences, most ghosts do not attack and very rarely show themselves. Not to say that none will, but Hollywood's portrayal of ghosts being violent and crudely disfigured is highly farfetched.

Q: Do you and your team members find that people expect ghosts to act or behave in a certain manner because of the way they are portrayed in the media?

Wayne Hackler: Many times, yes.

Gary Westerlund: Yes, most do expect stereotypical behavior. We educate them and hope it cures many of these thoughts.

Abbie Tippit: Absolutely.

Q: What do you and your team members do for fun?

Wayne Hackler: We each have our own way of having fun. For all of us, studying the paranormal is fun. Outside of the paranormal, I perform magic, scuba dive, and read and write as much as I can.

Gary Westerlund: I scuba dive, 4 wheel, do photography, build hot rods, tropical fish, and lots more.

Q: How do you think the ghost population of the Madison area compares with the rest of the nation?

Wayne Hackler: Hard to say. It would be great if there was a "ghost census" every ten years or so. Lacking that, I can't really say. I think in comparison to places that I've lived, I would have to say typical.

Gary Westerlund: Typical.

Q: What should you *avoid* doing when facing a ghost or what you perceive to be a ghost?

Wayne Hackler: Panic causes the majority of injuries. Keep your head, and if you need to leave an area, do so calmly without running.

Gary Westerlund: Being disrespectful, careless, acting scared or running.

Abbie Tippit: Never freak out and run. Although the typical ghost can't/won't hurt you, they can cause you to hurt yourself.

Q: Do you or your team have any personal or team encounters that you still think and talk about today?

Wayne Hackler: My experience at the outdoor location in Madison that I cited above for one. But several years ago, after my divorce, I was staying with my mom for a while. One evening, while I was lying on the couch watching TV, I was grabbed on my thigh. It was extremely painful. There was no one there, as I was the only one home. I noticed red finger marks on my leg that developed into bruises within a few hours.

Gary Westerlund: Yes, every time we meet we share those experiences and usually a new one will surface at our monthly meeting. Some are old and some very current.

Q: Please explain the process for requesting an investigation.

Wayne Hackler: People can email or telephone me and we'll get things rolling. Our Web site, www.madisonrip.com has our contact information.

Gary Westerlund: Contact us through our Web site and request an investigation. Wayne, our leader, will review it and make calls and decide if we need help or not.

Q: Please explain what a home or business owner might expect if you come to their home or place of business to conduct an investigation.

Wayne Hackler: They can expect us to be professional, compassionate, and thorough.

Gary Westerlund: When an investigation is done, we find out first if the person(s) want their information released, and if so, a form would be signed. We ask them if there are places we are not allowed. We tell them what each of us will be doing and that we

are very careful and respectful of their property. We also tell them how much time we need and ask if it is okay. We also explain we will go over our findings with them if there are any.

Research is 90% of what we do prior to, and following, an investigation. So *exciting* generally does not enter into the plan. There are long hours of investigating and even longer hours going through the info we get.

This is not for the thrill seeker or the impatient. We take this very seriously as we all have a lot of time and money involved in something that we do not charge for. It is not an exact science. We are continually learning more each day and from other teams' mistakes. There is so much more to be told and talked about, but time and paper limit us.

MRIP is changing attitudes one case at a time. Contact Wayne Hackler or any other member of Madison Researchers Into The Paranormal to learn more about them and what they do. Web site: http://www.madisonrip.com/.

What Kids Think About Ghosts

Left to Right: Cyndal Gilson, Cody Ferkey, Kennadie Jenner, and Jimmy Jenner. Not pictured: Makenzie Barron

Do you ever wonder what kids think about ghosts? I do. Kids are said to be more open to things of a paranormal nature, and said to be able to communicate more easily with the paranormal because they don't have any preconceived notions.

I also wonder if TV shows and movies dealing with ghosts and hauntings have had an effect on how kids perceive the world of the supernatural. I recently talked with five Wisconsin kids, ages 11-15, about ghosts: Makenzie Barron, 15, Kennadie Jenner, 12, Jimmy Jenner, 11, Cyndal Gilson, 12, and Cody Ferkey, 11.

Q: Do you believe in ghosts?

All said "yes" except Makenzie. However, later Makenzie changed her answer to: "I do, but I don't want to."

Q: Why do you think ghosts are here with us in the world of the living?

"They're relatives of people that are alive," says Kennadie Jenner. She also says, "They just didn't want to leave (this world)." Cody Ferkey believes some ghosts are here because they are "seeking revenge."

Makenzie has friends who live in a haunted house. She bases this statement on the fact that when you're in the house, you can feel breathing on the back of your neck and hear people talking who aren't there. She said lights turn off and on by themselves, too. She's also had a couple of strange personal experiences that she can't explain.

Once she was at her grandmother's house, upstairs watching TV. She decided to go downstairs to get something to drink. She remembers leaving the remote in a certain position and the TV on a certain station. When she came back upstairs, the remote was in a different position and the news was on TV. No one else could have changed the channel. She found it strange, but not too freaky.

She watched TV for a while and decided to go downstairs for something to eat this time. She made it a point to remember where she positioned the remote and what was on TV. When she returned the remote was not where she put it and the news, a different channel than what she had been watching, was on TV again.

She's had other experiences where she's heard voices and doors shutting and opening in her current home. She's been the only one there, but she doesn't attribute it to anything paranormal even though her mother, sister, and other relatives all believe there's something "strange" about the house.

Cyndal is Makenzie's sister, but has a totally different viewpoint when it comes to ghosts. Cyndal is in tune with things that most people don't pick up on. She's heard and seen things in her current home that she thinks could be caused by a ghost. She, along with her mother and others, think the house they live in is haunted by the former owners, an elderly couple. Many times, Cyndal has heard muffled conversations, though no one else is inside the house. Other times, the sound of a typewriter can be heard—and not only by Cyndal.

Cyndal can live with the conversations and the typewriter tapping; it's the dolls in the house that sometimes cause her to lose sleep. Her mother collects dolls, dolls that Cyndal considers borderline creepy. She thinks one doll is inhabited by a spirit and told me about a time her cousin slept over. She said she and her cousin both swear they saw the eyes of one doll move from staring straight ahead, to a sideways direction to look at them. She said she's happy that's all it did. Another time when Cyndal was alone in her room, the same doll, this time sitting on a miniature rocker, bent forward, turned to look at her, then immediately moved back the way it was.

Kennadie and Jimmy Jenner believe their house is haunted, but not all the time. They have both heard someone walk across the upstairs with distinct footsteps. Their mother has heard the same sound. Kennadie and Jimmy have both seen shadows appear in the window when there is no one there. When I mentioned several places in the town where they live, that are said to be haunted, I was stunned not only to learn that they knew about them—they also knew more about the ghosts than I did.

Cody Ferkey also knew about the haunted sites in town and also the stories behind the hauntings. He doesn't think ghosts are around all the time; he thinks they make an appearance for a reason. He told me about a time when he and his older brother, Eric, were alone at their home. They heard the doorbell ringing and went to see who it was. No one was there. As they shut the door, they heard a strange buzzing sound, and checked outside again. No one was there.

Eric locked the door, and he and Cody went downstairs to check the fuse box. Eric looked over the fuse box, and saw that everything was okay. As the two boys were about to walk upstairs, the fuse box fell away from the wall. They heard another buzzing sound and lights flickered. Both boys went back upstairs. After checking inside and outside again, they heard more noises.

Cody went with his brother back downstairs. This time the fuse box was the way it was the first time they had gone downstairs (against the wall) and the unit was closed. Cody isn't sure what caused those strange things to happen, but he doesn't rule out something supernatural.

The younger kids said a ghost might be "good," but it usually always scares you when it makes an appearance.

Madison Area Resources

Sources of Information

Listed below are just a few really great resources for information pertaining to Madison and the surrounding areas.

Greater Madison Convention and Visitor Bureau is the perfect place to learn about Madison and the surrounding area. Their Web site address is: http://www.visitmadison.com/. You can also call them: 608-255-2537 or 800-373-6376. The Welcome Center—Campus and Community Visitor Information is located at 21 N. Park Street in Madison. You can call them: 608-263-2400, or visit them on the Web: www.vip.wisc.edu.

The Wisconsin Alumni Association, 650 North Lake Street, Madison, WI 53706, phone: (608) 262-2552/(888) WIS-ALUM, has a large collection of UWM information, trivia, and really cool stuff. Read the ghost collection on their site: http://www.uwalumni.com/.

Historic Madison, Inc. http://www.historicmadison.org/. Contact the Historic Madison Cemetery Committee for more information about the historic cemeteries in Madison.

Dane County Historical Society: http://www.danenet.org/dchs/. You can visit them in person at the Lussier Family Heritage Center, 3101 Lake Farm Road in Madison, or give them a call: 608-224-3605.

Newspapers are a really great source of information about anything. In the Madison area, they are the *Isthmus, Madison Times, Onion, Badger Herald, Capital Times*, and the *Wisconsin State Journal*.

Milton Historical Society, Milton, Wisconsin.

Rock County Historical Society, 426 N. Jackson St., P.O. Box 8096, Janesville, WI, 53547-8096, (608) 756-4509, on the grounds of the Lincoln-Tallman House. Located on the Tallman Restoration grounds, the Wilson King Stone House contains the archival collection of the Rock County Historical Society. The library and office for the Rock County Genealogical Society is also located in the Stone house. For more information, visit the RCGS Web site at: *www.rootsweb. com/~wircgs/index.html*

City of Boscobel, Wisconsin, located at 1006 Wisconsin Avenue in Boscobel, WI 53805. Phone: 608-375-5001. They even have a toll free number: 1-888-710-5206.

Paranormal Groups and Sites of Interest

Contact Wayne Hackler or any other member of Madison Researchers Into The Paranormal to learn more about them and what they do. Website: http://www.madisonrip.com/.

Ghost Researchers In Madison (GRIM). Contact Terre Sims at terres123@sbcglobal.net, or (608)345-6477.

Heartland Paranormal Investigations (HPI). Most members are located in eastern Wisconsin: Kurt, Rhonda, Mark, and Chris are in Manitowoc, Krista is in Sheboygan, and Barry is in Richland Center. Website: www.heartlandparanormal.com.

Fox Valley Spirit Hunters (FVSH), located in east central Wisconsin in the Fox River Valley. Website: http://fvsh.sillybirds.com/.

Wisconsin/Illinois Paranormal Society (WIPS) is based in Illinois but serves Wisconsin and Illinois. Web site: http://www.w-i-p-s.com/.

Paranormal Investigators of Milwaukee (PIM) is based in Milwaukee. Web site: http://www.springcreeksoftware.com/pim/.

Confidential Paranormal Investigators (CPI). Web site: http://www. cpiteam.net/.

Greater Milwaukee Paranormal Research Group (GMPRG). Web site: http://www.gmprg-wi.com/.

Ghost Team Of Antigo. Web site: http://www.ghost-team-of-antigo.com/.

WIX, Wisconsin Paranormal Investigation Team, http://www.hauntedwi.com/.

Southern Wisconsin Paranormal Research Group. Web site: http://www.paranormalresearchgroup.com/.

Haunted Wisconsin, Ghosts of the Prairie. Web site: http://www.prairieghosts.com/hauntwi.html.

Haunted Places in Wisconsin. Web Site: http://theshadowlands.net/places/wisconsin.htm.

Madison Ghostseekers Society Homepage. Web site: http://hometown.aol.com/ssofsky/homeindex.html.

GhostTraveller. "Your Ghost Hunting Guide: Wisconsin. Web site: http://www.ghosttraveller.com/wisconsin.htm.

Wisconsinosity. Web site: http://www.wisconsinosity.com.

Selected Bibliography

Books, Magazines, & Periodicals

Allen, John. "On Wisconsin Ghost Stories." *On Wisconsin*. Wisconsin Alumni Association. UW-Madison. Fall 2006.

Birmingham, Robert A. and Eisenberg, Leslie E. *Indian Mounds of Wisconsin*. Madison, Wisconsin: The University of Wisconsin Press, 2000.

Birmingham, Robert A. and Goldstein, Lynne G. *Aztalan: mysteries of an ancient Indian town*. Madison, Wisconsin: Wisconsin Historical Society Press, 2005.

Boyer, Dennis. *Driftless Spirits: ghosts of southwest Wisconsin*. Madison, Wisconsin: Prairie Oak Press, 1996.

Erickson, Doug. "The Ghost Of The Old Baraboo Inn." Wisconsin State Journal. 5 July 2005.

Godfrey, Linda S. and Hendricks, Richard D. *Weird Wisconsin*. New York: Barnes & Noble Books, 2005.

Levy, Hannah Heidi and Borton, Brian G. *Famous Wisconsin Ghosts and Ghost Hunters*. Oregon, Wisconsin: Badger Books Inc., 2005.

Stark, William F. *Ghost Towns of Wisconsin*. Sheboygan, Wisconsin: Zimmerman Press, 1977.

Web sites

Allen, John. "On Wisconsin Ghost Stories." *On Wisconsin*. Wisconsin Alumni Association. UW-Madison. Fall 2006. http://www.uwalumni.com/home/pageswithouthome/onwisghosts/onwisghosts.aspx.

Brown, Charles E. "Lake Mendota Indian legends: prepared for the use of students, University of Wisconsin summer session." http://digital.library.wisc.edu/1711.dl/UW.MendLegends.

Buchel, John. "Madison a frequent haunt for ghosts." *The Badger Herald*. 29 Oct. 2003 http://badgerherald.com/news/2003/10/29/madison_a_frequent_h.php.

Cave of the Mounds. http://www.wisconsinhistory.org/.

City of Madison Parks. "Forest Hill Cemetery." http://www.ci.madison.wi.us/parks/forestHill.html.

Conrad, Eleanor and Tiedemann, Laurel. "Tour of East: a look inside." East Side High School. April 2007: 4-6.

Elsing, Vicky. I Am Haunted Paranormal Community. http://www.iamhaunted.com/Vicky-E.

GhostTraveller. "Your Ghost Hunting Guide: Wisconsin. http://www.ghosttraveller.com/wisconsin.htm.

Ghosts of America. "Wisconsin Ghost Sightings." http://www.ghostsofamerica.com/states/wi.html.

Haunted Places in Wisconsin. http://theshadowlands.net/places/wisconsin.htm.

Haunted Wisconsin, Ghosts of the Prairie. http://www.prairieghosts.com/hauntwi.html .

Historic Madison, Inc. http://www.historicmadison.org/.

Kowald, Joy. "Legends of paranormal." *Royal Purple News*. 31 Oct. 2007. http://media.www.royalpurplenews.com/media/storage/paper1225/news/2007/10/31/ArtsLifestyle/Legends.Of.Paranormal-3066612.shtml.

Madison Trust for Historic Preservation. http://www.madisontrust.org/.

Maternowski, Kate. "What lurks beneath the University of Wisconsin?" *The Badger Herald*. 13 Dec. 2006.

http://badgerherald.com/news/2006/12/13/what_lurks_beneath_t.php.

Milton House Historical Society. "Milton House Historical Museum." http://www.miltonhouse.org/index.html.

Monroe Chamber of Commerce and Industry. "Bed and Breakfasts..." http://wicip.uwplatt.edu/green/ci/monroe/guest/index.htm.

Salmen, Joanna. "Spooky ghosts possibly haunting Science Hall." *The Badger Herald*. 12 Nov. 2003. http://badgerherald.com/news/2003/11/12/spooky_ghosts_possib.php.

Southern Wisconsin Paranormal Research Group. http://www.paranormalresearchgroup.com/.

Spychalla, Luke. "Steam tunnels: Functional infrastructures, stuff of legend." *The Badger Herald*. 3 May 2002.

http://badgerherald.com/news/2002/05/03/steam_tunnels_functi.php.

Taliesen Preservation, Inc. http://www.taliesinpreservation.org/.

Western Wisconsin Camp Association, Inc. NSAC. http://www.campwonewoc.com/index.html.

The Wisconsin Historical Society. http://www.wisconsinhistory.org/.

Wisconsinosity. http://www.wisconsinosity.com.

WIX, Wisconsin Paranormal Investigation Team. http://www.hauntedwi.com/.

Index